COUNTRY ROADS
Albemarle County, Virginia

Susan De Alba

Rockbridge Publishing Company
Natural Bridge Station, Virginia

Published by

Rockbridge Publishing Company
Post Office Box 70
Natural Bridge Station, VA 24579
Telephone: 703-291-1063
Facsimile: 703-291-1346

Albemarle County General Highway Map copyright 1989
by the Commonwealth of Virginia, Department of Transportation,
adapted with permission.

Cover photo: Monticello by Hal Conroy

Library of Congress Cataloging-in-Publication Data

De Alba, Susan, 1944-
    Country roads: Albemarle County, Virginia / Susan De Alba.

    Includes bibliographical references and index.
    ISBN 0-9623572-1-9 (pbk.)
    1. Automobile travel—Description and travel—Guide-books. 2. Albemarle
County (Va.)—Description and travel—Guide-books. 3. Albemarle County (Va.)—
History.   I. Title
    GV1024.D4   1993
    917.58'48—dc20

                                                        91-31172
                                                          CIP

10   9   8   7   6   5   4   3   2   1
First Edition

Acknowledgments

Test drivers, both local history buffs and a few outlanders, ventured forth on early versions of these excursions and generously shared their knowledge and experience to make them informative and accurate. Others, arm-chair travelers, offered local lore and scholarship.

Special thanks to Elizabeth Coles Langhorne, Harry Langhorne, Howard and Barbara Newlon, Margaret O'Bryant, Melinda Frierson, Antoinette Roades, Lee Scouten, Lucia C. Stanton, Elizabeth Hobbs Fletcher, Alvaine Hamilton, Jim Wilson, Yvonne Farley, J. Randolph Conner, Ginny Lee, Lynn L. Neville, Richard F. Pietsch, Mrs. John LeGrand, Karen Hayden, Jenny Hayden, Bruce Hayden, John Page and Betty Williams, Lucy Werner, Sid Gray, Ann Carol Perry, Joseph E. Tolle, William and Walda Crapser, Charlene and Richard Nebel, Hervey E. Vigour, Natalie E. Ross, Ralph and Charlotte Damman, Muriel McMurdo, Jay Worrall, Jr., Janice Helmuth, Roy Barksdale, Kay Chretien, David Sagarin, and Don A. Swofford.

The Albemarle Historical Society and its wonderful archive was of great help. My thanks to the Charlottesville-Albemarle Visitor and Convention Bureau and its director, Bobbye Cochran, for setting this traveler on the road. And thanks, too, to Maynard Sipe, who verified the newly-assigned road names.

My daughter, Kate Snodgrass, fueled the project with her love of road trips and Blue Ridge history. My editor and publisher, Katherine Tennery, supported unflaggingly.

Contents

Introducing Albemarle County

Albemarle County lies at the center of the Piedmont of Virginia, a broad sweep of land rising from the fall line of the rivers to the crest of the Blue Ridge Mountains. Her scenic rivers drain pasturelands and ridges that cover deposits of granite, soapstone, slate and mica. The architects of Albemarle, many of whom also shaped our nation, surveyed this dramatic and verdant terrain, acquired land and settled here.

Beyond Charlottesville's urban crown of courthouse and university, nature still reigns. The county's country roads offer a legacy of scenes and stories to their travelers. Around any bend in the road a magnificent vista might make its bold claim, or a relic of a craftsman's skill or rural industry draw the traveler back in time.

The topography of the county, the mountain barriers and the natural passages of river-cut gaps and fords on rushing streams, explains the surface archaeology of roads, villages, plantations, taverns, mills and stores. Albemarle's beautiful landscape is studded with the largest collection of Jefferson-inspired neoclassical architecture in America and a plethora of other fascinating historic structures.

The tours in this book follow the old roads on their modern successors and will carry you through many levels of time as you explore this sublime, encompassing world.

A Little History

In the early 1700s, the Virginia Piedmont was an unoccupied Native American hunting ground, protected by treaty from English settlement. The indigenous Monacans, farmers and mound builders once feared by the coastal Powhatans, had already lost out to disease and war; the survivors had vanished, joining other tribes, like the Iroquois, whose hunting parties continued to pass along trails through the area.

About 1714, despite the treaty, Lieutenant Governor Alexander Spotswood decided to drive a wedge of English settlement into the Piedmont and block any future French or Indian efforts to claim it. Spotswood's 1722 treaty with the Iroquois moved their migratory trail to the western side of the Blue Ridge and set the stage for the unrestricted settlement of the Piedmont. Spotswood's own plantation and iron works on the Rappahannock River became the first of the new settlements, much to the displeasure of the James River planters who wished to move into lands along that river's western edge. Albemarle's territory remained out of bounds.

The opening of the James River Valley west of the falls at Henrico, now Richmond, was left to William Gooch, Spotswood's successor as governor. He created the vast county of Goochland in 1728. Between 1730 and 1750 every inch of the upland was claimed, the speed of settlement fueled by the bending of the colony's rules of land granting.

In Virginia's first hundred years, land was granted at 50 acres per planter; a man could claim this headright for himself and for each person he brought into the colony. By 1730 the council, made up of a few of the wealthiest planters, allowed favored individuals to purchase rights to thousands of acres from the government.

Albemarle, cut from the western end of Goochland in 1744, at first encompassed all of the James River Valley from the first mountains to the Blue Ridge. It was named for William Anne Keppel, earl of Albemarle, an absentee governor of Virginia (1737-54). Scottsville on the James was the county seat from 1745 to 1761.

In 1761 the part of Albemarle south of the James River was partitioned into new counties (Buckingham, Nelson, Amherst, much of Appomattox, part of Campbell), and the county seat was moved to Charlottesville. Fluvanna County was separated in 1777.

Albemarle is still a large county: 750 square miles, a rough trapezoid about 30 miles long by 25 miles wide. The Blue Ridge Mountains form the western boundary. The Southwest Mountains parallel the higher Blue Ridge a few miles inside the eastern boundary. In between are rolling meadows dotted with villages, beautiful estates, farms and the Ragged Mountains. Its heartland is crossed from west to east by the Hardware and Rivanna rivers; the James is the southern boundary.

The Roads

Between 1700 and 1780, nine time more land was taken up on Virginia's western frontier than was patented between 1607 and 1700 in all of Virginia. The roads kept pace, sweeping across the landscape with the speed of settlement. Section surveyors, appointed by the court justices from the landowners along the road, chose the sites. Neighboring planters and their laborers, many of whom were enslaved, built the roads and maintained them.

The 1731 River Road (US 6) followed the north bank of the James River westward from Richmond to its great horseshoe bend at

Scottsville. This road accounts for the quick settlement of the southern part of Albemarle.

Other settlers arrived via the Old Mountain Road (1733), which funneled them across Hanover County (north of Richmond), between the North and South Anna rivers, and into northern Albemarle, on the eastern slopes of the Southwest Mountains.

The most popular choice, after its vigorous development in the 1740s, was the Three Notched Road (variously spelled Three Notch'd and Three Chopt), also called the Mountain Road. It followed a ridge between the River Road and the Old Mountain Road and crossed the mountains through convenient gaps. It was so well-sited a road that US 250 follows it with little variation today; even I-64 is a close approximation.

North-south connectors were needed to link produce and people, especially to court and port at Scottsville on the James River. The Secretary's Road (1734), the Fredericksburg (Gordonsville) and Stony Point roads (1745) answered those needs. The Park Street/Rio Road link (1745) served the mills on the Rivanna River and carried commerce to the market at Charlottesville. The turnpikes chartered in the mid-1800s improved roads in use since the 1740s.

By the mid-19th century, the network of roads in Albemarle was largely complete, changing little until the population again began to grow in the 1970s. Even today the most heavily traveled routes closely follow their original sites. In naming the tours, historic names are used. On the maps accompanying the tours are road names assigned by the county in 1992.

The People

The terrain of Albemarle nurtured a remarkable group of political leaders influential beyond her bounds from the very beginning. Founders like Peter Jefferson, Joshua Fry, William Cabell and Charles Lynch were not great Tidewater planters, but counted among themselves recent immigrants, dissenters and former indentured servants. Surveyors and developers who derived power from their control of the land, and who were confident they could rationally manage their environment, they took charge.

Thomas Jefferson, born with his country, modelled his father: to explore, to map and to use the land well. Lifelong, Jefferson sought the beauty of his home terrain and found the pursuit of happiness was often the pursuit of land.

The golden age of Albemarle lasted from 1785 to 1850. Three men from the Piedmont dominated the American presidency from 1801 to 1825: Thomas Jefferson and James Monroe of Albemarle and James Madison from adjacent Orange County. Albemarle boasted four governors of Virginia between 1786 and 1831: Wilson Cary Nicholas, Thomas Mann Randolph, Edmund Randolph and Thomas Walker Gilmer; one U.S. senator: William Cabell Rives (1832-34 and 1836-45); and a speaker of the U.S. House of Representatives: Andrew Stevenson (1827-34).

Explorers and soldiers Meriwether Lewis, William Clark and George Rogers Clark, who changed the face and the shape of the early nation, were sons of Albemarle's pioneering families.

In more recent decades Albemarle has been home to people gifted in many fields, such as U.S. senator Thomas S. Martin, writers William Faulkner and Amelie Rives, U.S. Supreme Court justice John Blair and Virginia governors Colgate Darden and John S. Battle.

Before 1780, travelers were valued in an isolated frontier and welcomed into private homes. After 1780 the notion of personal privacy and the architecture that supported it flourished. Hospitality became more formal and less spontaneous. Jefferson often fled to his second home, Poplar Forest in Bedford County, to hide from the hordes who called upon him without warning at Monticello. Today privacy is protected by trespass law.

> Today's traveler is welcomed to Albemarle but advised not to drive down private lanes or enter historic properties that are private homes. These tours are written from a roadside point of view.

Included here are 14 tours, each based on historic roads. All driving instructions begin at the Thomas Jefferson Visitors Center on the Scottsville Road (VA 20), just south of the I-64 interchange (Exit 121). Some tours connect with others. Check the fold-out, master map at the back of the book to plan your trip. Each tour has one or more detailed maps of its own.

The mileage indicated at the head of each chapter is the mileage for that tour in one direction. It does not include the miles from your starting point (usually the Visitors Center) to the beginning of the tour, nor the return from the end of the tour.

Routes designated US (US 250, US 29) are federal highways. Those with a VA prefix (VA 53) are Virginia primary highways. Those with an SR designation are state secondary roads. Often these roads are narrow. Pull off if traffic build behind you; that will also give you time to read the history and descriptions of the area.

To see the roads as they existed in 1745, see Nathaniel Mason Pawlett's books, available from the Virginia Highway Research Council. A copy of the Green-Peyton map of 1875, which marks the location of houses by the name of the owner, can be purchased from the Albemarle Historical Society.

This collection of guided tours will set you on your way to discoveries—these and other enticing, historic roads of Albemarle. Bon voyage.

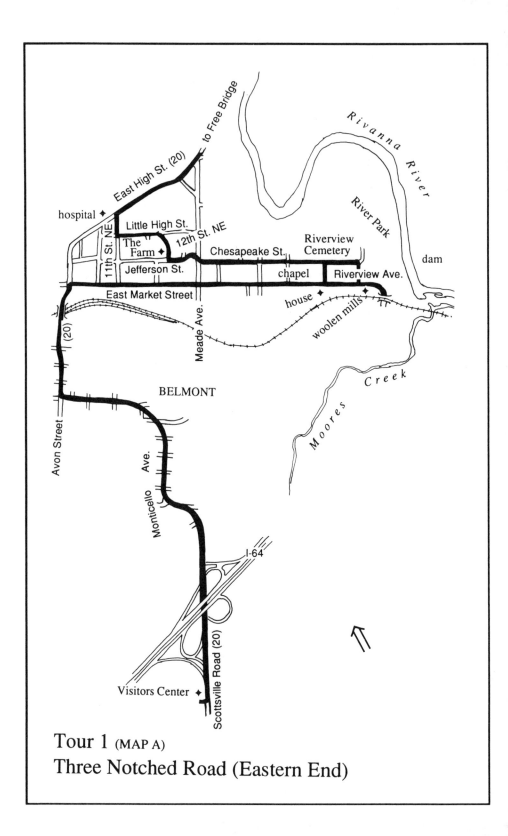

Tour 1 (MAP A)
Three Notched Road (Eastern End)

Tour 1   Three Notched Road (Eastern End)

From an historic commercial area to the
stagecoach stop at the county line: 14 miles

Named for axe blazes cut on trees that marked its path in 1742, the Three Notched Road was a heavily-traveled direct route between Richmond and the Shenandoah Valley. It crossed the first mountain ridge through the Rivanna River watergap and the river at Secretary's Ford, named for John Carter, secretary of Virginia in the 1730s, whose land met the gap.

At the traffic signal below the Visitors Center, turn left onto the Scottsville Road (VA 20). Just beyond I-64 begins a residential neighborhood called **Belmont.** Here VA 20 is called Monticello Avenue.

> Belmont, a Harvey and later a Ficklin farm, was subdivided at the beginning of this century to provide homes for the workers in the thriving mills and businesses along the nearby Rivanna River.
>
> Along the road are occasional catalpa trees with white blossoms in the spring and cigar-shaped pods in the fall and Asian ginkgo trees with large, heart-shaped leaves, offspring of trees Thomas Jefferson imported to Monticello.

Turn right at the traffic signal at Avon Street to follow VA 20 over the bridge that spans the railroad tracks.

Just beyond the bridge, turn right at the traffic signal onto East Market Street.

This part of East Market follows the path of the original Three Notched Road. In about a mile, the **Woolen Mills Chapel** marks the entrance to the **Woolen Mills** enclave.

The manager's house crowns the hill across from the chapel. The company provided a school, store, chapel (now the Rivanna Baptist Church) and brick duplex houses (some survive on the left) for the workers.

The mill itself, just ahead on the right, was housed in the three-story brick building now converted to residential use. Across the road is the dam that provided power to the mill.

Begun in the 1850s by John Adams Marchant, this building succeeds several generation of mills in this same spot. The first woolen cloth made here was used for slave clothing. During the Civil War, the mill made cloth for military uniforms.

In 1864 Marchant's war-crippled son, Henry Clay Marchant, bought the mill from his father and turned it into Charlottesville's leading industry. By the turn of the century, ninety percent of the nation's military school cadets, including those at West Point, and thousands of municipal employees and railway workers wore uniforms of cloth made here.

The mill operated into the 1950s. When it was sold in 1964 after a decade of decline, the neighborhood began to revive. A full renaissance occurred in the 1970s, thanks to restoration-minded residents.

Continue past the mill a few hundred yards and turn around at the railroad bridge, which crosses the river near Secretary's Ford.

Secretary Carter, son of acquisitive "King" Carter, controlled Virginia's lucrative land office, where patents could be obtained and ownership proved. He used his advantage to select for himself land destined for commercial development.

Backtrack past the mill, turn right on Riverview Avenue (at the church), then left on Chesapeake. The municipal **River Park,** which offers public access to the river, is at this junction.

On Chesapeake you will pass **Riverview Cemetery** (1790), one of the oldest in Charlottesville.

> Revolutionary soldier Nicholas Lewis (1734-1808) and Thomas Walker Lewis (1763-1807) are buried near the flagpole. Four old graves with head and foot stones are nearby.

> The tallest obelisk (between the entrance road and the flagpole) commemorates Confederate Major General Thomas Lafayette Rosser (1836-1910), who was so feared by the Yankees that General Philip H. Sheridan once ordered that the number of pickets were to be doubled if Rosser's men were nearby. During the Spanish-American War Rosser served as brigadier general of volunteers. He was an engineer for the Northern Pacific Railroad 1870-80 and chief engineer of the Canadian Pacific Railroad 1880-82. Later he was the postmaster of Charlottesville.

Continue on Chesapeake to the stop sign at Meade Avenue. Turn right and then immediately left onto Jefferson Street. In two blocks turn right onto 12th Street NE.

On the left, behind the high hedge, are two historic houses on what was once **The Farm,** a plantation of 1,020 acres that dates to the 1730s, when Nicholas Meriwether, the county's largest land patentee, made it part of his holdings.

> The larger house, the square brick Georgian that faces Jefferson, was built about 1830 by John A.G. Davis, a University of

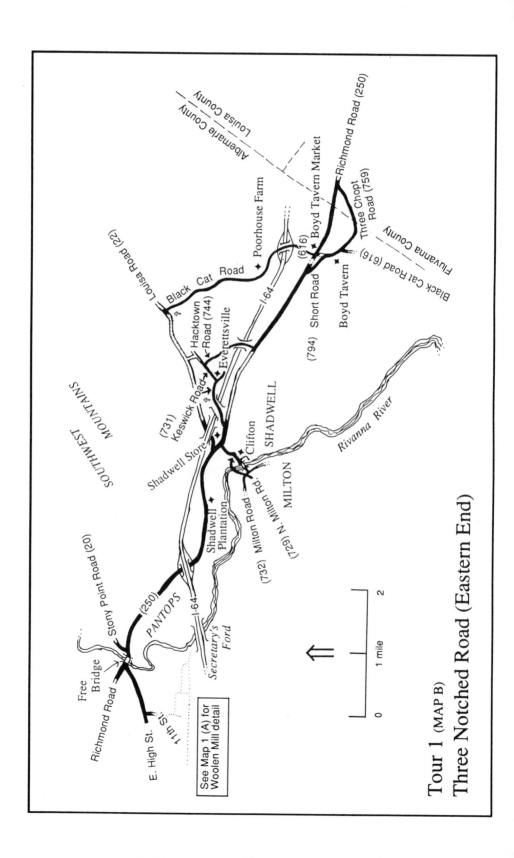

Tour 1 (MAP B)
Three Notched Road (Eastern End)

Virginia law professor and chairman of the faculty. In the 1830s, students had a penchant for rioting; Davis, attempting to restrain a student armed with a gun, was shot dead. This spurred the formation of the university's honor code.

The Farm was used as a sanitarium in the late 1800s. J.J. Browning, the first president of Martha Jefferson Hospital, once lived here.

The painted-brick house beside it (facing 12th), both smaller and older, was built by Colonel Nicholas Lewis and his wife Mary, who owned the plantation during the Revolution. Colonel Lewis was the uncle of explorer Meriwether Lewis and a close friend of Thomas Jefferson.

In June 1781, British Colonel Banastre Tarleton stopped here while in pursuit of Jefferson, then governor of Virginia, who had fled Richmond with other members of the legislature. Tarleton, known for his panache and charm, is said to have greeted Mistress Mary Lewis with, "Madam, you dwell in a little paradise." Mary, unfazed by his charm, reluctantly accepted her uninvited guests but pointedly gave Tarleton only her parlor floor for a bed and his dragoons the hard ground.

Continue on 12th to Little High Street and turn left. Turn right on 11th Street and go to the stop sign at East High Street (VA 20).

Look left on block to see the red brick **Martha Jefferson Hospital,** founded in 1903 by a group of physicians. Prior to the turn of the century, doctors performed operations in sanitariums located in their own homes.

Turn right on High Street, which was one of the posh residential neighborhoods following the Civil War. At the traffic signal at the US 250 bypass, turn right (east) and cross the **Rivanna River** on the **Free Bridge.**

The river is named for Queen Ann, the last of the royal Stuarts. Though narrow and shallow, not for deep-keeled boats, it permitted the movement of people and commerce though the long, otherwise unbroken ridge of the Southwest Mountains.

A ford here was bridged in 1801; that bridge was succeeded by a toll bridge in 1828, when the road was improved to turnpike status. A 1934 bridge, called "free" since a toll was no longer collected, was replaced by this bridge in 1992.

As you climb away from the river on the Richmond Road (US 250/VA 20), you enter land patented by Peter Jefferson, Thomas's father.

[Tour 3 begins on the left, where Stony Point Road (VA 20) heads northward; to continue this tour, remain on the Richmond Road.]

Peter Jefferson began his career as an assistant surveyor in Goochland County and then moved to Albemarle, where he eventually succeeded Joshua Fry as head surveyor. He and Fry mapped all of Virginia in 1751, the first comprehensive map since Captain John Smith recorded what he knew of the first settlement. The Fry-Jefferson map (1755) offered good details of the Piedmont and the mountains.

Jefferson's familiarity with the new country allowed him to select choice land for himself beginning in 1735. Here at the Rivanna watergap and ford, where the Three Notched and Fredericksburg roads eventually joined, he saw the potential for a trading complex with warehouses and mills.

The first of Peter Jefferson's farms is encountered on the eastern side of the Free Bridge. Its name, **Pantops,** lives on as a shopping center.

Peter's son Thomas, showing his youthful enthusiasm for all things Greek, named this farm with a Greek word meaning "all seeing." The land here rises sharply, and the view back toward Charlottesville and the mountains is, indeed, all-seeing. It is thought that Peter Jefferson was buried somewhere on Pantops when he died in 1757, a fitting resting place for a visionary who begot a visionary.

A mile east of the bridge, on the right and just past State Farm Boulevard, is a house that is called **Pantops.**

Built in 1938 for James Cheek of the Maxwell House Coffee family, today it houses the **Thomas Jefferson Center for the Protection of Free Expression.**

Beyond the I-64 interchange is the entrance to **Shadwell,** on the right, where you can pull off the road near the historical marker.

Shadwell, named for the London parish that was his wife's birthplace, was Peter Jefferson's home plantation. He acquired land here in 1735, but the large tract did not include the house site, which adjoins the river. He bought that 200 acres from his best friend, who was also his wife's first cousin, William Randolph, for the "consideration" of the largest bowl of Arrack punch at Wetherburn's Tavern in Williamsburg. He built a house about two years later.

Thomas Jefferson was born at Shadwell on April 13, 1743. The family moved to Tuckahoe, near Richmond, in 1745 to care for William Randolph's orphans and returned to Shadwell in 1752. The house burned in 1770, destroying Peter Jefferson's papers and Thomas's library. Thomas then moved to Monticello, where he had already built a small pavilion.

The Thomas Jefferson Memorial Foundation, which owns the site, has conducted archaeological studies there.

[In a little less than a mile is the junction with Louisa Road (VA 22). Tour 4 begins there, at the **Shadwell Store,** but you will continue east on US 250 to see the rest of Three Notched.]

Just past the Shadwell Store, turn right onto North Milton Road (SR 729). In a scant half mile, just before you reach the bridge, turn left on an unmarked lane that dead ends at a public access point on the river, the site of the now-vanished **village of Shadwell,** across the river from the nearly-vanished **town of Milton.**

Milton was established on the shallows of the Rivanna River in 1789; as the northernmost navigable point on the Rivanna, by the mid-1790s it was equal in size to Charlottesville and even more important commercially.

Between 1801 and 1817, Thomas Jefferson bought much of the land surrounding Milton; he thought its future bright. Jefferson's first mill, which stood west of the bridge, was destroyed by a flood in 1771; he rebuilt it 1803-06. Never a success, by 1853 it was again in ruins.

Canals and dredging improved access from the James River to this port after 1805, and by 1815 it was one of the three main trading centers in Albemarle. Here were some 25 houses, a public tobacco warehouse, a post office and general trading facilities. Shadwell (or North Milton), rivaled the original settlement by 1835. It boasted a wool carding factory with 100 employees, a large merchant mill, a saw mill, several general stores, shops and dwellings.

Milton's day in the sun was short-lived because the canals were not kept in repair and unimpeded access to the James was never assured during the rest of the 19th century. Ultimately, rails and new roads bypassed Milton an guaranteed its demise. The old Three Notched Road followed the river's edge on this, the Shadwell side of the river.

Backtrack to the Richmond Road, past **Clifton,** a bed and breakfast inn included in the National Register of Historic Places.

Clifton was originally part of William Randolph's Edgehill plantation. It was later owned by Thomas Mann Randolph, a governor of Virginia (1819-22) who was Thomas Jefferson's son-in-law.

In this section US 250 does not follow the original Three Notched road bed, but, fortunately, some little-trafficked secondary roads do, and they are wonderfully nostalgic of early Albemarle. Turn right on Richmond Road and then left on Keswick Road (SR 731).

Keswick Road crosses over I-64. On the left, watch for the **Union Run Baptist Church.**

The church was named for a nearby stream that was a favorite camping spot for the wagoners hauling produce to Milton. The stream eventually became known as Camping Branch, but the church name remained unchanged.

About a half mile beyond the church, where Keswick Road turns sharply to the left, in the area known as **Everettsville,** is a beautiful stuccoed Greek Revival house.

Originally a tavern on Three Notched Road, this building stood on the Belmont plantation of Col. James Harvie, Jefferson's guardian. Dr. Charles Everett, a prominent Philadelphia-trained physician, bought 1200 acres of the plantation from Harvie. Everett served briefly as President James Monroe's private secretary. He later opposed Jefferson's party, but nevertheless he treated Jefferson in his last illness.

At his death in 1848, Everett's nephew and heir, Dr. John Everett, honored his uncle's will by freeing Everett's slaves. He later supported the Confederacy with a loan of $110,000—a sizeable fortune never repaid him. After the Civil War, the house served travelers as La Fourche Tavern.

Since the old Three Notched is blocked, follow Keswick Road past the house, then turn right onto Hacktown Road (SR 744) and follow it a couple of miles to US 250.

Turn left (east) onto US 250 for two and one half miles and bear right onto Short Road (gravel, SR 794) for half a mile, then bear right onto Blackcat Road (SR 616).

Here the original three Notched Road met the old stagecoach road (now Blackcat Road), which connected it to the old River Road to Richmond.

In three tenths of a mile, on the right, **Boyd Tavern** stands at Blackcat Road's junction with Three Chopt Road (SR 759).

This tavern, one of the many taverns and stables on the stagecoach route, was built in 1780 for Thomas D. Boyd, rebuilt in 1868 after a fire, and renovated in the 1970s as a private residence.

Near here in 1781, the marquis de Lafayette's troops prevented Cornwallis from reaching military supplies stored in Albemarle. The marquis revisited Boyd Tavern during his grand reunion tour of the United States in 1824. Local dignitaries, self-proclaimed the Lafayette Guard, met him here to escort him to Monticello for a moving reunion with Thomas Jefferson.

Beyond Boyd Tavern, bear left on Three Chopt Road. It is a little more than a mile to US 250 (where we leave the original Three Notched Road on this tour). Turn left (west) onto US 250 and drive about a mile to the quaint **Boyd Tavern Market.**

This rural store, built in 1935 and restored, retains the best of the old while accepting the new. It offers its neighbors and travelers a convenience store with snack, grocery and deli items, a post office, video rentals and gas pumps.

Just west of the store, turn right onto Blackcat Road (SR 616). In about a mile a white board fence marks the boundary of the **Poorhouse Farm,** now a private residence, that can be glimpsed from the road.

About 1840 a log schoolhouse was opened here by Mrs. Joshua Wheeler, still in her teens. The students were children from the mountains, and their tuition was paid by the county's Indigent Fund for Poor Whites.

The farmhouse is the essence of the clean, straightforward style and natural sense of proportion of the local carpenters. This old farm has a wonderful accretion of outbuildings.

About five miles past the Poorhouse Farm, look for the **South Plains Presbyterian Church** on the left, opposite Belcourt Farm. The church was built in 1827-28 and altered in the 1850s.

Just beyond the church is the junction with Louisa Road (VA 22). Tour 1 ends here. To return to Charlottesville, turn left on Louisa Road and then right (east) onto US 250 a couple of miles to the south.

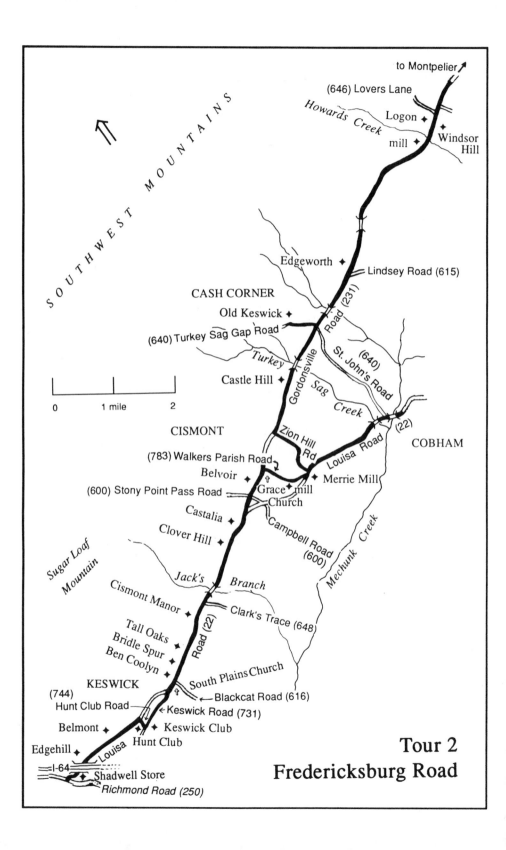

to Montpelier

(646) Lovers Lane

Howards Creek

Logon

mill

Windsor Hill

S O U T H W E S T   M O U N T A I N S

Edgeworth

Lindsey Road (615)

CASH CORNER

Old Keswick

(640) Turkey Sag Gap Road

Road (231)

St. John's Road

(640)

Turkey

Gordonsville

Castle Hill

Sag

Creek

0   1 mile   2

CISMONT

Zion Hill Rd

COBHAM

Louisa Road

(22)

(783) Walkers Parish Road

Belvoir

Merrie Mill

(600) Stony Point Pass Road

Grace Church

mill

Castalia

Campbell Road (600)

Clover Hill

Mechunk Creek

Sugar Loaf Mountain

Jack's

Branch

Cismont Manor

Clark's Trace (648)

Tall Oaks

Bridle Spur

Road (22)

Ben Coolyn

South Plains Church

KESWICK

(744)

Blackcat Road (616)

Hunt Club Road

Keswick Road (731)

Belmont

Keswick Club

Edgehill

Louisa

Hunt Club

I-64

Shadwell Store

Richmond Road (250)

Tour 2
Fredericksburg Road

Tour 2   Fredericksburg Road

From Peter Jefferson's 1730s Shadwell
Plantation to Montpelier: 14 miles

The Fredericksburg Road dates to the 1730s. It runs on the eastern edge of the Southwest Mountains, the first natural barrier to travelers from Hanover and Louisa counties as they moved westward into Albemarle's territory. Eventually the Louisa, Gordonsville and Fredericksburg roads linked to make a major commercial thoroughfare.

Imagine wagons laden with tobacco or corn groaning ponderously toward Fredericksburg or rough ambulances bearing Confederate wounded bumping painfully toward the hospitals in Charlottesville. Think, too, of exuberant boys like Thomas Jefferson riding their ponies to a cooperative school on one of the larger plantations, remnants of which remain clearly evident.

As you leave the Visitors Center, turn left on the Scottsville Road, then left again to enter eastbound I-64. Get off at Exit 124 (the next exit), turn right (east) on Richmond Road (US 250) and go two miles to the **Shadwell Store.**

[You may also reach this point by following the beginning of Tour 1 to the Shadwell Store.]

Bear left where the Louisa Road (VA 22), part of the Old Mountain Road, forks north from Richmond Road. High on the hill to the left, just beyond the I-64 bridge, look for the remarkable barn of the **Edgehill** plantation, built in 1790.

William Randolph patented this land in 1735, and it became home to a succession of illustrious Randolphs, including Governor Thomas Mann Randolph and his son, Thomas Jefferson Randolph, whose wife Jane was the daughter of Albemarle-born governor Wilson Cary Nicholas.

With her daughters, Jane started a school for young women on the estate in 1836 to help support the family as her husband struggled to pay off his father's and grandfather's debts.

Within a half mile, on the left, is the entrance to **Belmont,** one of the oldest plantations in the county.

Scotsman John Harvie, another close friend of Peter Jefferson, bought 2500 acres here in 1730. His son, John Harvie II, was a member of the Virginia legislature and the Continental Congress; he won for Albemarle the dubious honor of hosting a prisoner of war camp in the Revolution and later headed Virginia's land office.

Turn right on Hunt Club Road (SR 744) to see the **Keswick Hunt Club** (1896), beyond the old show grounds.

At the turn of the century, this was the horseman's mecca in Albemarle. The Hunt is still quite active and headquartered in this charming setting, a piece of tradition cheek-by-jowl with thoughtful modern development.

Turn lest on Keswick Road (SR 731) at the entrance to the **Keswick Country Club and Inn.**

Sir Bernard Ashley, who with his late wife founded the internationally-known Laura Ashley company, is creating a bed and breakfast inn with golf community out of the 1920s Keswick Country Club grounds.

Continue on Keswick Road past the new horse show grounds and across the one-lane bridge to the heart of **Keswick.**

Local lore has it that the name of this district derives from Nicholas Meriwether's ancestral home in England or the birthplace of the popular romantic poet Robert Southey. The first use of the name was for Thornton Rogers's farm, on which the depot was built in 1850.

On the right are the spacious grounds of **Little Keswick,** a residential school for boys with learning disabilities.

The red brick train depot that once served a spur of the main line still announces your arrival in Keswick Station. The coming of the railroad transformed this area of Albemarle, giving it fast, reliable access to urban centers such as Fredericksburg, Washington and New York. From its earliest days, Keswick attracted sophisticated and rich visitors. After 1848 they came by train, and many became residents.

General Sheridan burned the depot in 1865 as he raided Confederate supplies and supply lines in the Piedmont. This is the third station, built in 1909.

Stop here for a few minutes to read about the **Clarksville plantation,** coming up next. Several points of interest appear in quick succession, and you won't have time to look and read once you're back on busy Louisa Road.

Christopher Clark was the 60-year-old patriarch of an extended family of Quakers who settled on the eastern slopes of the Southwest Mountains beginning in 1742. He established the Clarksville plantation on the southern part of a 14,000-acre tract he had patented in 1727, the year of Albemarle's first patents, in partnership with Nicholas Meriwether, a fellow justice from Hanover County.

The Clarks and other Quakers had organized a meeting by 1749 (on the north side of Sugar Loaf Mountain, northwest of here), though being dissenters from the established state church, they risked legal discrimination. The family moved to Bedford County in 1754, where the next generation founded Lynchburg. By the Revolution, the Quaker element had all but vanished from Albemarle, though some of its democratic ideas persisted.

Clark's grandson, William Clark, inherited Clarksville. He apparently left the Quaker meeting because he was a justice of Albemarle's court before his death in 1800, a position requiring the taking of an oath, an act objected to by Quakers. His widow, Elizabeth Allen Clark, operated an ordinary at Clarksville considered by travelers to be "an excellent house of entertainment."

Clarksville was eventually divided among various descendants and sold out of the family. Not far ahead you will see the romantic entrances to three farms: **Ben Coolyn** (which means breezy mountain), **Bridle Spur** and **Tall Oaks,** all once part of the much larger holding.

Turn right on Louisa Road. In just one tenth of a mile, at the junction with Blackcat Road (SR 616), is the small, red brick **South Plains Presbyterian Church** (1827-28), on the right. The entrance to Ben Coolyn is on the left.

"Plains was a popular designation for local Presbyterian churches, being offshoots of the first one, Mountain Plains. Jefferson noted the momentum of conversions before the Revolution that made the majority of Albemarle residents followers of Calvin rather than the Church of England.

Continue northward past **Cismont Manor** (1760), also on the left. You are now within the bounds of Nicholas Meriwether's larger share of the land patented in partnership with Clark. By 1730, Meriwether had patented a total of 18,000 acres, making him the largest landholder in the area.

> For the sake of comparison, the average Piedmont farm in 1790 was 260 acres. About half of the white males owned land, and just over 10% of them held more than 500 acres.

> The fact that Meriwether and Clark were able to claim and hold this much land reflects their political clout (both were lawyers and county court justices in Hanover County) and the state's desire to settle the Piedmont as quickly as possible.

> Cismont Manor was cut from Clover Fields, the Meriwether farm north of it. Christopher Clark's house was moved here in 1820 to begin a new life as a kitchen, a typical recycling of the early houses.

Beyond Cismont Manor is the intersection with **Clark's Trace** (SR 648), cut by Christopher Clark to connected the eastern Quaker communities along the Old Mountain Road to their meeting house on Sugar Loaf Mountain. It was the first road to enter the mountains.

Jack's Branch is a creek thought to have been named for a freed slave who lived nearby.

North of Jack's Branch you will pass farms cut from the original tract for Meriwether descendants between 1830 and 1850 and little altered since. They include **Clover Fields, Clover Hill** and **Castalia,** all private homes hidden from the road.

Beyond Castalia, bear left onto the Gordonsville Road (VA 231). This little community is called **Cismont,** Latin meaning "this side of the mountain."

This junction is near the end point of the Old Mountain Road. When settlers arrived, they cut roads northward to Gordonsville and ultimately to Fredericksburg.

A later crossroads village was called **Bowlesville** for William Bowles, a mid-19th century spinner and weaver who apprenticed orphans to his craft. A store and a few houses on Stony Point Pass Road (SR 600) are all that remain of a number of stores, homes and a smith.

As you continue northward on the Gordonsville Road, you are passing **Belvoir,** another of the Meriwether estates, on the left. The entrance is on Stony Point Pass Road.

Belvoir descended to John Walker, a boyhood friend of Thomas Jefferson. Once, when Walker was away at an Indian conference, the young Jefferson offered his affection to his friend's wife. Years later the Federalist couple opposed Jefferson's bid for the presidency and made the most of the indiscretion when the press made it public during the campaign.

Belvoir eventually came to Walker's granddaughter, Eliza Kinloch. She married Hugh Nelson, the son of Virginia's Revolutionary governor Thomas Nelson, who was a federal judge, a member of Congress 1811-23 and a minister to Spain under president James Monroe.

In about seven tenths of a mile, on the right, is the **Grace Episcopal Church.** Turn right into the churchyard for a good look.

The Anglican church had a role in governing on the local level. The vestry was, in certain respects, a court of law, and every resident of the parish paid a tax to support the church and the poor of the parish, much to the dislike of the Quakers and Presbyterians. The Fredericksville parish, which served the northern half of the county, was formed in 1742.

As early as 1724 there was a small mountain chapel on this site, called Walker's or Belvoir church. The first church was built in 1760. A later church (1848-95) burned. Its crenelated tower and four walls were incorporated into the 1896 reconstruction, funded by Walker descendants, which you see here. The 1600-pound, 1848 bell was saved and rings each Sunday.

The Blessing of the Hounds, a tradition in some English villages, was adopted here in 1928 and continues today. Members of the Keswick Hunt, astride their best mounts and attended by their hounds, meet the rector and onlookers in front of the church on Thanksgiving morning for the ceremony.

Just beyond the church, turn onto Walkers Parish Road (SR 783, a well-graded gravel road). If you look back toward the church, especially in winter, you will see a scene worthy of William Wordsworth, Walter Scott or Robert Southey, poets much admired by this church's builders.

Continue about a mile down this forested road to the impressive remnants of **Merrie Mill,** built by John Walker of Belvoir. It is massive, four and a half stories, and the stone is beautifully laid.

Two tenths of a mile beyond the mill the road ends at the Louisa Road. The estate across the road is also called **Merrie Mill.**

In the early 1900s, it was the home of John Armstrong Chaloner, a wealthy lawyer whose eccentricities led his family to commit him to a mental hospital for four years. His return to Albemarle brought a degree of excitement to the countryside. Chaloner held extravagant Fourth of July celebrations for the local folk and had the first movie theater in the county, housed in a barn and free to all comers.

On one memorable occasion his neighbor's wife sought refuge at Merrie Mill from her husband, who was beating her. Chaloner shot him, then commemorated the place of death by inlaying a giant star in the dining room floor.

Turn left onto Louisa Road, being very careful at this almost blind junction, and drive into the tiny community of **Cobham** on **Mechunk Creek,** at the junction with St. John's Road (SR 640).

Cobham took its name from a farm owned by William Cabell Rives, Jr., a Meriwether-Walker descendant; the farm was named for a town in Surrey, England.

Mechunk Creek (which has been paralleling our route, on the right and out of sight, from near Keswick) was named for the only member of the Monacan tribe encountered by Captain John Smith in 1607. Mechunk described the geography and settlements of his people to Smith, who recorded that information on his map of Virginia.

The Monacans were Siouxan speakers, unrelated to the Algonquins (Powhatans) in eastern Virginia, and probably were more powerful because they controlled the trading of the copper that both tribes valued. Smith talked to many Powhatans but on one Monacan, which skewed his interpretation of tribal power in favor of the Powhatan confederacy.

From Cobham, backtrack on Louisa Road, and turn right on Zion Hill Road (SR 740).

Turn right again when you reach the stop sign at Gordonsville Road, and go just over a mile to the historic marker (on the right) opposite **Castle Hill.** Stop there to read the next few paragraphs.

You may catch a glimpse of the house high on the mountain to your left in winter; foliage hides it in summer. The original house, a modest story-and-a-half clapboard, was built in 1764. A second house, brick with Tuscan portico, was built in 1824. The two buildings are wed, and the marriage, though incongruous, works. It was rare in Virginia that in building a newer, grander house, the old one was retained as a major element.

Nicholas Meriwether, a grandson of the original patentee Nicholas Meriwether, was the first of the family to settle here. His widow, Mildred Thornton Meriwether, married Thomas Walker of Fredericksburg, a physician. Walker managed his wife's portion of the Meriwether property, still in the thousands of acres, providing farms for their eleven children and her daughter by Meriwether.

Walker was the first Englishman to explore the Virginia territory beyond the Allegheny Mountains. In 1750 he led a party of six into the area that is the present-day state of Kentucky. The French and Indian War interfered with the settlement of the area, and the treaty that ended the war restricted settlers beyond the Appalachian divide to those with military service. This remained the rule until after the Revolution, obscuring Walker's role in the opening of Kentucky.

In Walker's day, Castle Hill was a stopping place for notables like Peter and Thomas Jefferson and Logan, a Mingo chief known for his great oratory.

It was from here that Walker left for the treaty conference with the Six Indian Nations that resulted in the purchase of six million acres in the west, nearly all of Kentucky and Ohio, in 1777.

In 1781, Walker delayed British Colonel Tarleton at Castle Hill with a lavish breakfast, giving Jefferson and the Virginia legislators time to escape capture in Charlottesville.

Walker's granddaughter Judith married William Cabell Rives; they built the 1824 brick house. Rives served in the U.S. House of Representatives and in the U.S. Senate, was twice a minister to France and once minister to England.

Their daughter, Amelie, a writer, eventually inherited Castle Hill. Her first novel, a best seller in 1888, was *The Quick and the Dead.* It portrayed the sexual nature of her characters, and though it scandalized some, it drew favorable comments from Henry James, Oscar Wilde and Thomas Hardy.

After an unsuccessful marriage to John Armstrong Chaloner of Merrie Mill, Amelie married Prince Pierre Troubetskoy, a Russian painter whom she met on one of her grand tours of Europe. Oscar Wilde supposedly introduced them, wanting to see what would happen when the "two most beautiful people in London" met.

Take to the road again and drive about 2.5 miles beyond Castle Hill to **Cash Corner.** Turn left onto Turkey Gap Road (SR 640), which dates to the earliest period of county history. Go about a half mile to catch a glimpse of **Old Keswick,** on the right, from its entrance gate.

Old Keswick was once Thomas Walker's hunting lodge, called Turkey Hill, and dates to the mid-1700s. The old lodge was gracefully encased in clapboard when it was enlarged in 1815-18 by Walker's granddaughter, Jane Frances Page and her husband, Dr. Mann Page.

Education was a Page passion. Between 1830 and 1895, Old Keswick was a school for boys. Generations of Pages taught at the University of Virginia; James Morris Page was dean there for thirty years. His three sisters, like characters from Jane Austen, lived here in cultivated isolation.

The estate is now a breeding farm for thoroughbred racing stock. It is the birthplace of Elnawaagi, who was sold to the ruling family of Dubai in 1964 for a record $4 million.

Return to the Gordonsville Road and turn left. Mechunk Creek flows beneath the bridge just past Cash Corner. Continue northward 1.4 miles to **Edgeworth,** on the left, once the glebe of Grace Episcopal Church.

A glebe was home to an Anglican minister, the farm that provided the produce that supplied his living. This 400-acre tract was donated to the church in 1753 by Nicholas Meriwether. The original Edgeworth house burned in the 1830s.

The Reverend James Maury, grandfather of scientist and naval officer Matthew Fontaine Maury (1806-73), served the church from 1754 until his death in 1770. He kept a classical school for boys near the glebe, which Thomas Jefferson attended.

It was the Reverend Maury who brought suit in the Parson's Cause, the case that propelled Patrick Henry to fame. In 1759 the clergy, whose salaries had been much reduced by an act of the legislature, petitioned the court for relief. The British Privy Council disallowed the act, and the clergy then sued to recover their back salaries. The jury agreed that the act was "no law," but swayed by Henry's great power of oratory, they returned a verdict of just one pence back pay to Maury, an empty victory indeed.

About 2.2 miles north of here, watch for a low point in the road, on a curve. On the left are the remnants of a mill, circa 1821, which are easy to miss. (Easier to spot on the return trip.)

This is **Walker's Mill** on **Howard's Creek,** once called Cowherds in honor of a later mill owner.

Just across the creek, on the right, is an 1850s brick mansion, **Windsor Hill.**

> At the turn of the century, this was the home of James Gavin Field (1826-1901), who practiced law in Culpeper after he lost a leg in the Civil War. He served as attorney general of Virginia (1877-82) and despite his Confederate past ran for vice president of the U.S. on the populist's People's Party ticket in 1892. He married Miss Cowherds, who lived here.

On the left is an estate called **Logan,** named by Thomas Walker for his Indian friend.

> Logan was a Cayuga, a Shawnee tribe that was part of the Iroquois confederacy. Born in 1725, he was named for James Logan, Pennsylvania's Indian negotiator. Converted to Christianity by Moravian missionaries, and a friend to white settlers, he refused to join Pontiac against the English in the French and Indian War.

> In 1774 a group of Ohio frontiersmen, armed and backed by George Rogers Clark for frontier defense, killed a group of peaceful Native Americans that included Logan's wife, his children and other family members. Logan claimed 30 scalps in his bid for revenge and was captured by Virginia troops at the battle of Point Pleasant. He spoke in his own defense:

> "I appeal to any white man to say if ever he entered Logan's cabin hungry and he gave him not meat; if ever he came cold and naked and he clothed him not. During the course of the last long and bloody war, Logan remained idle in his cabin, an advocate for peace. Such was my love for the whites, that my countrymen pointed as they passed and said, 'Logan is the friend of white men.' I had even thought to have lived with you, but for the injuries of one man. Col. Cresap, last spring, in cold blood and unprovoked, murdered all the relations of

Logan, not even sparing my woman and children. There runs not a drop of my blood in the veins of any living creature. This called on me for revenge. I have sought it. I have killed many. I have fully glutted my vengeance. For my country I rejoice at the beams of peace, but do not harbor a thought that mine is the joy of fear. He will not turn on his heel to save his life. Who is there to mourn for Logan?—Not one."

The speech was widely reported in 1775, and many children in Virginia were named in his honor, including some in Albemarle. Jefferson was so impressed that he recorded the speech in his *Notes on the State of Virginia* as evidence of Native American oratorical skill.

Walker's son built a home west of Logan, which he named Indian Fields for its use by the local Monacans. It cannot be seen from the road.

This is the end of our tour. The county line is about six tenths of a mile north of Logan. Reverse your route to return to Charlottesville.

If you wish to extend you journey, continue north about 13 miles into Orange County to **Montpelier,** home of President James Madison and his wife, Dolley Payne Todd Madison, who often used this road to visit Jefferson, Monroe and other friends in Albemarle. To reach Montpelier, follow the Gordonsville Road into Gordonsville, then take US 15 to Orange and follow the signs.

For the stout-hearted explorer: You may take Turkey Sag Gap Road or Stony Point Pass across the Southwest Mountains and return to Charlottesville via Stony Point Road (VA 20). These uncivilized roads give a sense of the wilderness in which the early arrivals pursued their lives and livelihoods. Be warned, however, that these unpaved secondary roads are narrow and steep in spots and may be a challenge to drive.

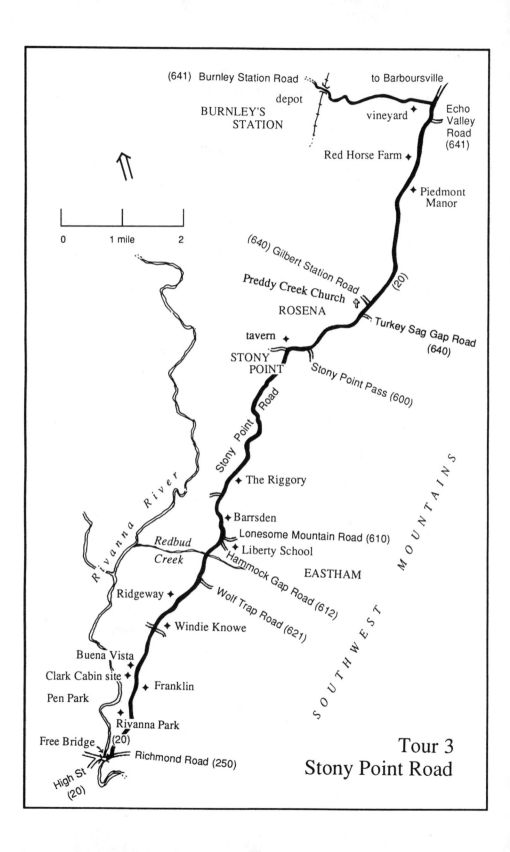

(641) Burnley Station Road · · · ·   to Barboursville

depot   Echo
BURNLEY'S   vineyard ✦   Valley
STATION   Road
                                               (641)

                    Red Horse Farm ✦

                              ✦ Piedmont
                                 Manor

(640) Gilbert Station Road

Preddy Creek Church ⇧   (20)

ROSENA   Turkey Sag Gap Road
                                          (640)
tavern ✦

STONY
   POINT   Stony Point Pass (600)

                Stony Point Road

          ✦ The Riggory

          ✦ Barrsden
          Lonesome Mountain Road (610)
          ✦ Liberty School

Redbud   EASTHAM
Creek   Hammock Gap Road (612)

Ridgeway ✦   Wolf Trap Road (621)

          ✦ Windie Knowe

Buena Vista
Clark Cabin site ✦
Pen Park   ✦ Franklin

   Rivanna Park
Free Bridge   (20)
          Richmond Road (250)
High St
  (20)

Rivanna River

SOUTHWEST MOUNTAINS

0   1 mile   2

Tour 3
Stony Point Road

Tour 3   Stony Point Road

From Pantops to Barboursville: 19 miles

Stony Point Road, first called Coursey's Road, crossed the Southwest Mountains via Stony Point Pass, followed the Rivanna River to the Stony Point settlement and continued to Secretary's Ford near Charlottesville. Later it was extended to Barboursville.

From the Visitors Center, follow the Scottsville Road (VA 20) through Charlottesville, and turn right on Richmond Road (US 250). Just beyond the Free Bridge, turn left on Stony Point Road (a continuation of VA 20) at the traffic signal.

[For information about the points of interest between the Visitors Center and this point, see Tour 1, pages 9 to 14.]

In half a mile, turn left into **Rivanna Park,** just past the **Elks Club.** Where the paved road turns right to the parking lot, turn left on the gravel road, toward the river. Drive up the hill and look westward to view **Pen Park,** another public park across the river.

> In the 18th century the Stony Point Road crossed the river here via a ford, later improved to a ferry by Charles Lynch, an Irish immigrant who grew wealthy via land speculation.
>
> Northward, on the river bank but out of sight, is a niche in the rocks called Indian Seat. Tradition identifies it as a ceremonial meeting place for Native Americans of the area.

Return to Stony Point Road and turn left. In half a mile, on the right, is **Franklin,** the home of Benjamin Franklin's grandson, Dr.

William Bache. The house is most easily seen in winter. Turn right on the road just beyond it for a better view.

Bache bought the house in 1799 on Thomas Jefferson's recommendation, but his residence in Albemarle did not last long. He was considered an incompetent physician, failed to develop a regular medical practice and lost Franklin to Thomas Randolph in a lawsuit in 1804. Bache left Albemarle to take a government position in New Orleans. Legend has it that Meriwether Lewis stayed at Franklin when he served as secretary to President Jefferson.

Continue north on Stony Point Road. In a third of a mile (just past Dorrier Drive), pull off on the left side of the road to see the **Clark cabin site.**

A small house is identified as George Rogers Clark's birthplace. This is not the original cabin, but an 18th-century miller's house moved here from near the Gordonsville Road as part of the 1976 U.S. bicentennial celebration. It stands on a foundation discovered by Ashton Edward McMurdo, who owned the farm in the first half of this century. McMurdo felt sure this was the site of Clark's cabin because the foundation was close to a good spring.

George Rogers Clark's father, John Clark, owned a 400-acre farm here, cut from the original grant of 3,000 acres patented by his father, Joseph Clark, and several partners. The John Clarks left here when George Rogers was a small boy.

In 1772, 20-year-old George Rogers Clark led an exploration party to survey land beyond the Alleghenies. A year later, his family settled in Kentucky, on fine bottom land near the Ohio River. A younger son, William Clark of the Lewis and Clark Expedition, probably was born there.

In the Revolution, George Rogers Clark commanded four companies of American soldiers against the British in a fight to control the old Northwest Territory (between the Alleghenies and the Mississippi, from the Ohio River all the way to Canada). On July 4, 1778, Clark and his 175 men surprised the fort at Kaskaskia, captured the British general and his garrison and, after some give and take, secured the territory.

Pull up to the stone entrance to **Buena Vista,** a Greek Revival house built in 1862, a rare building project accomplished in Virginia during the Civil War. McMurdo built the beautiful stone and wood barn behind the house after he purchased the farm in 1883.

In half a mile, on the right, is the entrance to **Windie Knowe.**

> The was a Key family grant; their property included Franklin and a mill. Tradition says this was a 1732 hunting lodge, making it a contender for the oldest Albemarle house. It was reportedly the scene of much carousing.

Just beyond Windie Know, on the left, is the **Chapman Grove Baptist Church,** founded by black residents, many of whom were the descendants of slave families.

> This 1955 church replaced a turn-of-the-century structure. A school for black children stood next door in 1910, one of the first public schools for blacks in the county.

Half a mile farther, on the left, is the entrance to **Ridgeway,** the 1809 home of Peter Minor, treasurer of the Rivanna Navigation Company and secretary of the progressive Albemarle County Agricultural Society. The house, unfortunately, cannot be seen from the road; please do not enter the grounds.

> Minor was a partner of Cyrus McCormick of Rockbridge County, inventor of the McCormick reaper, in the manufac-

turing of agricultural machinery. McCormick provided Minor with a skilled mechanic, who built a furnace and forge here for making the mould board ploughs that Minor sold.

Peter Minor's son, Franklin, for a time operated at Ridgeway a well-respected classical school, which he moved here from The Riggory, another estate held by the family.

Continue north about a mile. Here you will see two right turns in quick succession, Hammock Gap Road (SR 612) and Lonesome Mountain Road (SR 610). This is **Eastham,** an old hamlet on **Rosebud Creek.** Between the two roads is the **Liberty School,** closed in 1938 and now a private residence.

Built in 1919 as a gift of Paul Goodloe McIntire, it was a two-room elementary school for the children of the area. Along Lonesome Mountain Road the many trees planted by the students in various Arbor Day celebrations.

As you continue north on Stony Point Road, you are passing through part of Major Thomas Carr's patents of 1730-37, which reached west to the hamlet of Proffitt, two and a half miles away.

Once of the Carr farms is **Barrsden;** look for its entrance on the right, although the main house cannot be seen from the road.

In winter, when the trees are bare, you may be able to see a small clapboard house if you look down the private driveway. It is one of the few slave cabins that remain the county; it has been renovated.

Beyond Barrsden, the 1829 **Liberty Baptist Church** sits on a knoll above the road, also on the right.

The only Carr house easily seen from the road is **The Riggory,** half mile north of Barrsden. It was built in 1796 by John Carr.

In the next two and a half miles the road twists through woods and along a stream.

> Many of the farms along this section of Stony Point Road supplied grapes to the Monticello Wine Company after Adolph Russow planted a vineyard in 1872 at nearby Belvue. Russow was superintendent of the company that was the largest seller of wine in the United States before prohibition.

Where Stony Point Road makes a 90-degree turn to the right at the junction with Stony Point Pass (SR 600) are the remnants of **Stony Point.** This community was established as early as 1740 at the western end of Stony Point Pass.

> At the turn is a quaint tavern and an abandoned store. Some early houses are scattered among the more modern homes across from the 1935 **Stony Point Elementary School.**

As you leave Stony Point, the tiny, wooden **All Saints Episcopal Chapel** is on the right.

> Grace Church at Cismont (at the eastern end of Stony Point Pass) established this chapel mission. It was built 1926-29 at a cost of $1736. A three-year-old girl, Nancy Feaganes, was killed by a stone that rolled from one of the nearby mountains; it became the cornerstone and is engraved, "Except ye be converted, and become as little children, ye shall not enter the kingdom of heaven."

In about 1.3 miles, a convenience store welcomes you to **Rosena,** a town forgotten but for this friendly commercial reminder.

> Directly opposite the store is Turkey Sag Gap Road (SR 640) which crosses the mountains following Turkey Sag Creek through Turkey Sag Gap beside the Turkey Sag Mountain.

Just beyond the store, on the left, is the **Preddy's Creek Baptist Church,** clapboard on a stone foundation and dating to 1781.

This church is material evidence of the second Great Awakening, a religious revival that swept the country following the Revolution.

Continue on Stony Point Road about a mile to the 1850 **Piedmont Manor,** surrounded by miles of white cross-barred fences.

The house looks straight out of *Gone with the Wind.* It did star in the movie "Virginia" with Fred MacMurry and Madeleine Carroll. Parts of "Giant" with Rock Hudson, Elizabeth Taylor and James Dean were filmed here also.

Rev. James Walker Goss moved his school for girls here from Gordonsville in 1851. He had known the area as a child, when his father was minister of the Preddy's Creek Baptist Church. James founded the Market Street Disciples Church in Charlottesville.

Ahead half a mile, on the left, **Red Horse Farm** has several pretty old houses to see from the road. This farm is identified as Green Plains on the Green-Peyton map.

The landscape here is open; pastures roll eastward up Peters Mountain, named for Peter Jefferson, and wide vistas open out to the distant Blue Ridge to the west.

In about two miles, turn left on Burnley Station Road (SR 641), an old road that snakes across the northern edge of Albemarle. In about half a mile is **Burnley's Vineyard,** which welcomes visitors April through October.

Continue two mile to **Burnley's Station,** an old depot community on the Southern Railroad.

A modern one-lane bridge over **Burnley Creek** announces the village. A picturesque, one-lane wooden bridge arches over the railroad track. Cross the bridge and turn left to see the old depot, now an artisan's shop.

Return to Stony Point Road and continue north two miles to the **Barboursville Winery** in Orange County. Bear right on the Old Barboursville Road (SR 738) at the lumber yard. Turn right on Governor Barbour Street (SR 678) and right again on Vineyard Road (SR 777) to the ruins of the **Barboursville plantation.**

Architectural historians consider Governor James Barbour's 1822 home Thomas Jefferson's most beautiful design.

The house caught fire on Christmas Day in 1884 while the family was at dinner. When it was clear that the fire could not be controlled, the story goes, they moved the dining table out to the lawn and finished their meal. The ruin resonates with romance and vanished grace. It is fun to see the substructure, usually hidden in great houses, here laid out skeletally.

While here you can picnic and tour the winery, owned by the Zonin family, vintners from northern Italy. Jefferson loved northern Italy's neoclassical villas and her wines. In 1976 the Zonins planted the first *vitis vinifera* in the state, successfully reviving Jefferson's dream for winemaking potential in the Virginia Piedmont.

Retrace your route to return to Charlottesville.

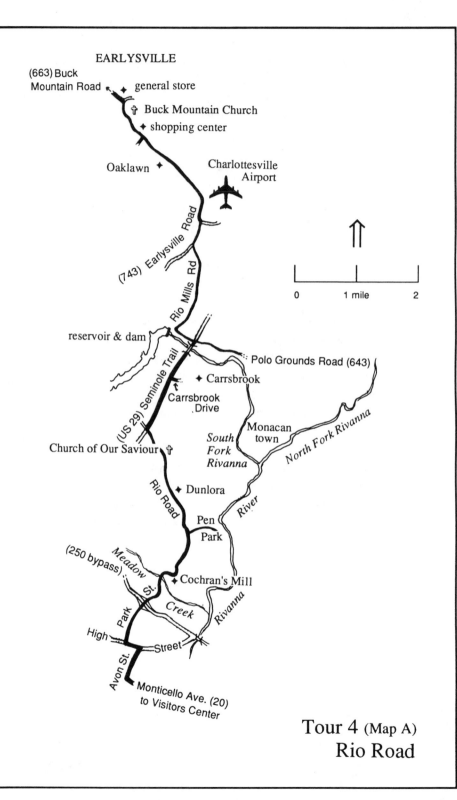

EARLYSVILLE

(663) Buck
Mountain Road   ✦ general store

✝ Buck Mountain Church

✦ shopping center

Oaklawn ✦

Charlottesville
Airport

(743) Earlysville Road

Rio Mills Rd

reservoir & dam

0   1 mile   2

Seminole Trail

Polo Grounds Road (643)

✦ Carrsbrook

Carrsbrook
Drive

(US 29)

Monacan
town

Church of Our Saviour ✝

South
Fork
Rivanna

North Fork Rivanna

Rio Road

✦ Dunlora

River

Pen
Park

(250 bypass)

Meadow St.

✦ Cochran's Mill

Rivanna

Park St.

Creek

High   Street

Avon St.

Monticello Ave. (20)
to Visitors Center

Tour 4 (Map A)
Rio Road

Tour 4   Rio and Buck Mountain Roads

From Charlottesville to Earlysville and
Boonesville: 25 miles

The Rio and Buck Mountain roads carried rural tradesmen between Charlottesville and the wild and mountainous northern corner of Albemarle. Through those mountains came Stonewall Jackson's army, in one of his highly successful secret maneuvers. Along the way we'll track the embarrassed General Custer as he retreats from Charlottesville.

[Note: Tours 4, 5 and 6 connect to form a loop about 40 miles long through northwestern Albemarle. They may be combined for a pleasant circle tour.]

From the Visitors Center, follow VA 20 north about two miles, then turn left onto High Street (the second traffic signal after the bridge over the tracks). In three blocks, turn right onto Park Street.

For about a third of a mile, Park Street passes through an area of Charlottesville rich with 19th-century homes representing a variety of architectural styles.

> At 713 Park, on the left, is the graceful brick home (1861) of Judge Egbert R. Watson, a friend of president James Monroe.

Park Street crosses over the US 250 bypass as it heads for the city limits. Beyond the **Park Street Christian Church** you'll cross **Meadow Creek.** The second driveway on the right past the bridge is the entrance to **Cochran's Mill,** an old miller's cottage and mill that houses an antique shop.

The mill dates to 1754. John Cochran owned it in 1829. The wooden upper part of the mill burned in 1941 and the stone foundation was roofed over.

Park Street became Rio Road when you crossed Meadow Creek. The origin of the name Rio (pronounced rye-oh) has been much speculate upon; it is most likely a variation or abbreviation of Rivanna, the nearby river.

Continue on Rio Road and turn right into **Pen Park,** a pleasant municipal golf course and general recreation facility. Follow the road to its end.

The **Rivanna River** curves around the golf course. On the opposite bank is the farm where George Rogers Clark was born.

Charles Lynch, the original owner of Pen Park, came to Virginia as a servant indentured to Christopher and Penelope Clark, founding members of the Quaker Meeting in the county. Lynch eventually married the Clarks' daughter and became a successful land speculator. His wife, it is thought, named the Lynch home for the most famous Quaker in America, William Penn, the founder of Pennsylvania. Lynch won court approval in 1744 to operate a ferry over the Rivanna River from his plantation.

George Gilmer owned Pen Park on the eve of the Revolution. Gilmer, who led a citizens' committee formed in 1774, is called the Sam Adams of Albemarle because he was zealous for rebellion. When Virginia's royal governor, John Murray, earl of Dunmore, removed the munitions from the magazine in the capital, 1st Lieut. Gilmer of the Albemarle Volunteers and 27 of his compatriots marched to Williamsburg to join other militia units in protest.

In the late 19th century, William Hotopp owned Pen Park and was influential in the development of the Monticello Wine Company.

Leave the park and turn right onto Rio Road.

In a quarter mile, on the right, you will pass the entrance to Dunlora Plantation, a modern subdivision named for the Carr estate established here in 1730.

Sir Thomas Carr of King William County patented 5,000 acres in Albemarle between 1730 and 1737. Thomas Carr's grandson, Dabney, was Thomas Jefferson's best friend. Dabney married Jefferson's sister Martha, and the couple eventually inherited Dunlora. When Dabney died on the threshold of a promising political career, Jefferson took the Carr family under his protection at Monticello. Jefferson's nephew, Samuel Carr, inherited Dunlora and made it his home.

Beyond Dunlora, Rio Road passes some service stations and small stores. The pretty stone chapel just beyond the commercial section is the Episcopal **Church of Our Saviour.**

Turn right at the traffic signal on Seminole Trail (US 29). In about a mile turn right on Carrsbrook Drive. Take the second left, Marlboro Court, to Gloucester Road (second right) to its intersection with Gloucester Court (a left turn) to see **Carrsbrook,** the only remaining Carr family home.

This beautifully preserved home is a Virginia Historic Landmark, but it is privately owned and not open to the public. It sits very close to the road and can be seen easily in winter, when no leaves block the view.

The five-part house approaches the classical style that Jefferson favored; it is caught half way between the old and the new, combining the Colonial "I" and neoclassical three-part designs.

Peter Carr built the house about 1794 and lived here until his death in 1815. He attended William and Mary College and played an important role in the founding of the University of Virginia, providing able assistance to his uncle, Thomas Jefferson. Peter is often mentioned by historians as the likely father of the mulatto children born to Sally Hemings, a Monticello slave. His brother Samuel is less often suggested.

Return to the Seminole Trail and turn right. Cross the Rivanna River, then turn right onto Polo Grounds Road (SR 643). In exactly one mile, stop at roadside near the landscape nursery. The south branch of the Rivanna River is marked by the natural tree line behind the orderly rows of cultivated young trees.

Jefferson's *Notes on the State of Virginia* recounts his excavation of a Monacan burial mound on the south branch of the Rivanna River near here. His was the first scientific archaeological excavation using a trench system. He estimated that two thousand bodies had been buried in successive layers over a long period of time, each layer covered with dirt and stones.

Jefferson was unaware that this mound was near *Monasukapanough,* a town of some significance. The town occupied both sides of the Rivanna above the river's fork, near the US 29 bridge. There are at least 63 and perhaps as many as several thousand sites of Native American habitation along rivers and streams in Albemarle County; this is an important one.

Such settlements had vanished from Albemarle by 1700, but Jefferson noted that in his lifetime a party of Monacans found their way unaided to the mound site, though they had to hike six miles from the main road to locate it. Once they found the mound, they stayed near it for some time, with expressions interpreted as sorrowing.

There were several other mounds in the forks of the Rivanna, in an area commonly called the Indian Graves Low Lands, about two miles from here.

Return to US 29 and continue across it to Rio Mills Road (SR 643, unpaved). In three tenths of a mile, where the road makes a 90-degree turn to the right, turn left up the dead end paved road to view the **hydroelectric dam** on the Rivanna River.

On February 29, 1864, Union general George Armstrong Custer, on a mission to destroy Confederate supplies, unexpectedly encountered a Confederate detachment camped south of Rio Mill (across the river, near the dam). Custer's cavalry rode in among the soldiers just rising for breakfast, thus setting the stage for the Rio Hill skirmish.

Although Custer had between 1,500 and 3,000 soldiers (estimates vary), he believed he was facing a formidable foe because the few Confederates on the hill, directed by a quick-thinking junior officer, made a show of noise and activity. They circled forward and pulled out of sight again and again, thus appearing to be a formidable force. The Confederates were part of J.E.B. Stuart's horse artillery battalion in winter encampment under the temporary command of Captain Marcellus M. Moorman.

As Custer withdrew to the north, near where you are now, he destroyed the Rio Mill and burned miller Nathaniel Burnley's bridge over the Rivanna. Charlottesville felt enormous gratitude to the small band of defenders and fêted the heroes. The mill and bridge were rebuilt, only to be destroyed by a great flood in 1870.

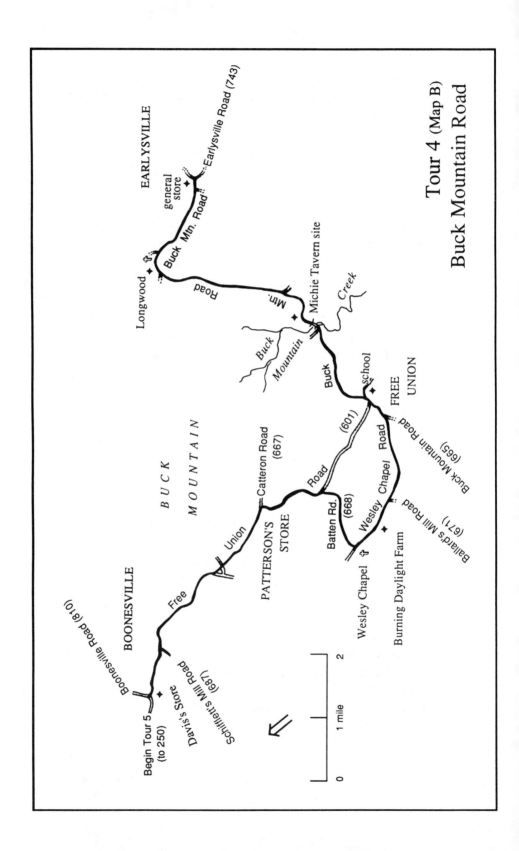

Tour 4 (Map B)
Buck Mountain Road

Follow the gravel road 1.5 miles to its junction with the Earlysville Road (SR 743). Turn right toward Earlysville.

As you pass the airport, you are following the route of the original Buck Mountain Road, also called Earlysville Road once there was a town. This tour follows the old road from here to Free Union, a little over nine miles in all.

About two miles from the turn, in a wooded area on the left, Custer and his men stopped at **Oaklawn,** the Twyman family home. The house cannot be seen from the road.

George Twyman built his home in 1750, and his descendants inhabited Oaklawn until 1965. During their visit, Custer's men kicked in the doors of handmade cupboards in a desperate search for food. The Yankees moved on, the war ended, and the Twymans were left with nothing but their house with its empty cupboards.

The last of the family, a spinster and her four bachelor brothers, were born at the end of Reconstruction, but the poverty of the family was still unrelieved. Their simple agrarian lifestyle did not provide the cash they needed to participate in the developing industrial society. Proud and self-sufficient, they carried on without electricity, indoor plumbing, telephone or automobile.

Just ahead, on the right, is the Earlysville Green Shopping Center, where there is a restaurant.

Beyond the commercial center, behind a low stone wall, is the **Buck Mountain Church,** a Virginia Historic Landmark.

This church is one of three built in 1747 to serve the Fredericksville parish of the Anglican church. It originally stood two miles west of here, on the Buck Mountain Road.

After the Revolution, when the Anglican church was disestablished as the state church, this building was abandoned. A rejuvenated parish repurchased the church in the 1860s, dismantled it and rebuilt it on this site. The church is smaller than before but retains most of its original framing, weatherboards and interior trim. It is a rare example of the early, simple wooden Anglican churches.

In a short distance, bear left onto Buck Mountain Road (SR 663) at the **Earlysville General Store** in the heart of the old village.

Earlysville was named for John Richard Early, who lived here, and the Early-Durette family, who lived north of here. The village, as well as the whole county, took pride in distantly-related Confederate general Jubal Early.

The village has changed little since 1835, when it was described as having a tavern, wheelwright, tanner, blacksmith and tailor in addition to a general store and seven houses. Population then: 35. Population 1990: 828.

About a mile and a half from the store, bear left at the **Chestnut Grove Baptist Church** (1773) to follow Buck Mountain Road (now SR 664).

This is the oldest continuous Baptist congregation in Albemarle. It used the Buck Mountain Church building after the Revolution until it was repurchased by the Anglicans.

Just around the next curve, behind the boxwood hedge on the right is **Longwood,** a Michie family home.

The Scottish John Michie (pronounced Mickey) bought about 1,200 acres here in 1748 from John Henry, Patrick's father. A third-generation Michie, Beau Jim, was a go-getter who ran a store and a post office at Longwood.

Beau Jim's son succeeded him and became a doctor, apothecary, storekeeper and postmaster. He opened an apothecary across from the university and supplied medicines to doctors all over the Piedmont. Following the Civil War, he lost his battle with the economy and had to sell Longwood at auction.

Bear left again just beyond Longwood to stay on the Buck Mountain Road (here SR 665) as it wends through former Michie lands.

The original site of Michie Tavern is about a half mile past the Hickory Ridge subdivision. The tavern stood on the high ground above the **Buck Mountain Creek,** which you will cross in about half a mile. The tavern was relocated in 1927 and now serves the public near Monticello.

Free Union, a mile and a half beyond the creek, was once known as Nixville. Turn left on Free Union Road (SR 601) to see the **Free Union Country School,** just ahead on the right.

Built in the 1980s, the school combines two old log cabins, which provide a scale and atmosphere perfectly suited to the education of the children living in this beautiful landscape.

Beyond the school is a modern (1962) church that houses a Church of the Brethren congregation that dates back to the 1730s.

The Brethren, commonly called Dunkards by the non-Brethren, were "plain people" of German heritage who were anti-slavery pacifists and outstanding farmers. Their missionaries came to Albemarle from the Shenandoah Valley and set up meeting houses in Jarman's Gap, Sugar Hollow and Brown's Gap. This church, founded in 1895, is an offshoot of the Locust Grove Church in Brown's Gap.

Return to the junction with Buck Mountain Road and turn left. Bear left again to continue on Buck Mountain Road past the **Free**

Union Baptist Church. The congregation existed prior to 1833, and the building is at least 100 years old.

Bear right past the church on Wesley Chapel Road (SR 609/671).

> Here you leave the historic Buck Mountain Road, which continued south to White Hall, although historians are uncertain of its exact path beyond this point.

In a mile and a half you will see the white fences of **Burning Daylight Farm,** a small thoroughbred breeding and training operation, and enjoy some of the loveliest mountain views in the county.

Almost a mile past Burning Daylight, on the left, is **Wesley Chapel** with its old cemetery.

> Worship services were first held in William S. Thompson's tobacco barn. In 1833, the Methodists built this chapel on land bought from Nathaniel Thompson by church trustees Brightberry Brown and Thomas H. Brown of Brown's Cove. Some Gothic-style changes were made later. The Methodists shared their worship hall with the Baptists in the early years.
>
> When Confederate general Stonewall Jackson came through Brown's Gap on his way to the railroad depot at Mechums River in May of 1862, some of his men rested in the shade of the trees and camped on the grounds. The wounded who died here are buried in the cemetery; no graves are marked.

At the chapel, turn right on Chapel Springs Lane (SR 668, gravel) and follow it about 1.2 miles to Free Union Road (SR 601). Look to the left from Chapel Springs Lane for your first glimpse of **Buck Mountain.**

Turn left onto Free Union Road to continue toward Boonesville.

This road skirts Buck Mountain, which rises to the right.

The quality of the landscape changes, becoming wilder and more mountainous, with breathtaking views. Scattered cabins suggest the early Scotch-Irish mountaineers who were by and large isolated in this then-remote section of the county.

Around the junction with Catteron Road (SR 667) is a cluster of tidy little buildings known as **Patterson's Store.**

In about four miles there is a jewel of a country store at the junction with the Boonesville Road (SR 810). This is **Boonesville,** named for Daniel Boone.

Here is the prettiest country store in Albemarle. The building, pristine and small, has wonderful touches like the diagonal boards of the double front door, a double porch with fancy trim and, inside, its original cage. It is the oldest store building in the county.

The cage, a barred partition securing a section of the store, had its origin in taverns, where the innkeeper kept his valuable spirits under lock and key and dispensed drinks through a barred window in his storeroom. (Hence "bar" for a place to buy alcoholic drinks.) After Prohibition, when stores no longer sold spirits, the cage was used to secure the post office, records or valuable stock.

This is the end of Tour 4. To continue the three-tour loop back toward Charlottesville, turn to Tour 5.

For the most direct return to Charlottesville, backtrack on Free Union Road (SR 601). It eventually becomes Barracks Road and meets US 250 just west of US 29, at the city limits (about 16 miles away).

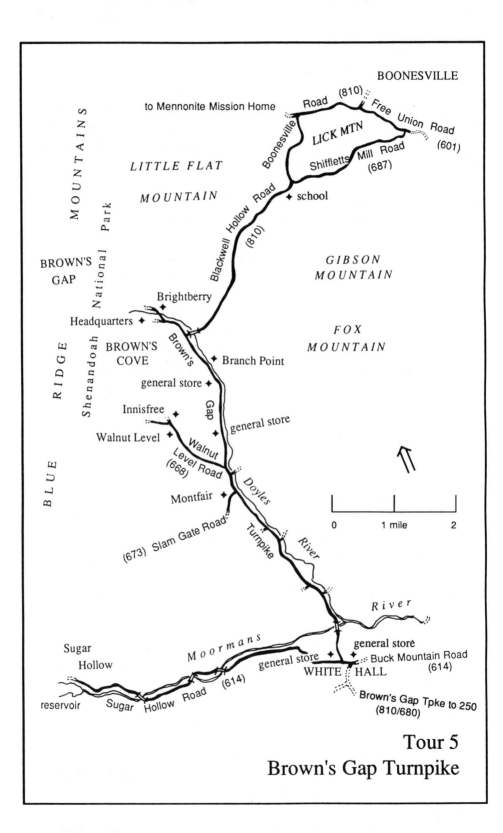

BOONESVILLE

to Mennonite Mission Home

Boonesville Road (810)

Free Union Road (601)

LICK MTN

Shiffletts Mill Road (687)

LITTLE FLAT

MOUNTAIN

Blackwell Hollow Road (810)

✦ school

M O U N T A I N S

GIBSON MOUNTAIN

BROWN'S GAP

Shenandoah National Park

Brightberry ✦

Headquarters ✦

BROWN'S COVE

Brown's Gap

✦ Branch Point

general store ✦

FOX MOUNTAIN

Innisfree ✦

Walnut Level ✦

Walnut Level Road (668)

general store

Montfair ✦

Doyles

(673) Slam Gate Road

Turnpike

River

B L U E   R I D G E

0   1 mile   2

R i v e r

Sugar Hollow

M o o r m a n s

general store

general store ✦ ✦

WHITE HALL

Buck Mountain Road (614)

reservoir   Sugar Hollow Road (614)

Brown's Gap Tpke to 250 (810/680)

Tour 5
Brown's Gap Turnpike

Tour 5   Brown's Gap Turnpike

From Boonesville to White Hall: 8 miles

Tucked close to the base of the Blue Ridge, the oldest turnpike in the county (1806-1930) follows Doyles River as it meanders through an isolated wilderness. Every bend in the road holds a promise of adventure, from carefully hidden moonshiners to reportedly haunted mansions.

[Note: this tour links tours 4 and 6. See master map inside back cover.]

To get to Boonesville from the Visitors Center, take I-64 west to the US 29 bypass north (exit 118B), and exit the bypass at the third exit, Barracks Road. Turn left (west) on Barracks Road, which eventually becomes Free Union Road (SR 601). Note that the road makes a 90-degree right turn at the Hunt Country Corner Store. Boonesville is about 16 miles from US 29.

Once in Boonesville (described on page 53), there are two ways to begin the tour, a direct and a scenic route.

DIRECT ROUTE: go left (south) on Boonesville Road and then Blackwell Hollow Road (both SR 810). About a mile from Boonesville look for signs for the Mennonite Mission Home, where exceptionally tasty baked goods can be purchased if you want to make a little side trip. Note the junction with Shiffletts Mill Road (SR 687) as you pass it in about 2.3 miles

SCENIC ROUTE: go south one mile on Free Union Road (SR 601) and turn west on Shiffletts Mill Road (SR 687), a lovely, unpaved byway. This five miles is one of the most beautiful passages in the mountains as it follows Muddy Creek (which isn't muddy at all). The changing mountain vistas offer many visual delights. Turn left when you get to Blackwell Hollow Road (SR 810).

A tenth of a mile south of the junction of Blackwell Hollow and Shiffletts Mill roads, in **Blackwell's Hollow,** was a school for young boys with special needs dating to the 1930s.

> Boys Haven, more recently known as Adventure Bound, can be identified by its two beautiful stone buildings and a clapboard chapel. It closed in 1992.

The landscape is dramatic and grand in this pocket valley tucked inside the Blue Ridge Mountains.

> Although you are but a handful of miles from a major city, there are only a few signs of civilization, and even they don't intrude overmuch. During Prohibition, when the government agents went looking for moonshiners, this area was a good place to scout.

> The cluster of mountains to the left is collectively called **Fox Mountain** (Gibson, Martins and High Top are included). **Loft** and **Little Flat Mountain** are to the right.

About three miles past Blackwell Hollow the road makes a 90-degree turn to the left at the junction with the Brown's Gap Turnpike (SR 629). This is **Brown's Gap,** named for a Welsh family.

Turn right and drive a few hundred yards on the Brown's Gap Turnpike, following **Doyles River,** to see **Headquarters** (1769), one of the Brown family homes.

> Captain Benjamin Brown and his wife Sara, landholders from Hanover County, acquired 8,000 acres here, east of the

mountain pass that linked Albemarle and Augusta counties, between 1747 and 1760.

Benjamin had a large family; among his sons were Benjamin, Jr.; Billy; Bartlett; Bernard; Bernis; Benajah; Barzallia (or Barzillai); Bezaieel (or Bazaleel) and Brightberry.

Bazaleel was an aide to George Washington. Bernard, a dispatch rider between Charleston and New York in the Revolution, was known for his speed and agility in slipping through the enemy lines. Bernis is credited with successfully hiding the Virginia archives when the legislature fled Richmond. Billy and Bartlett settled in South Carolina.

Brightberry was known for his engineering skills. It was he who built Headquarters, and he operated a sawmill, tannery and furniture factory here. His nephew, Thomas Harris Brown, also a woodworker, was known for his grandfather clocks and for the artificial limbs he perfected for maimed veterans of the Civil War.

The unexpected elegance of the house, found at what was nearly the end of the world when it was built, makes it one of the most romantic houses in Albemarle. In the attic of the brick wing are boards dated 1769, 1782 and 1784. The frame section was built in 1818 to replace a much earlier part that burned.

Brown's Gap, cut by the Doyles River, west of the houses, was a well traveled natural passage, a logical place for the industrious Brightberry to build a turnpike.

In 1805, Brightberry and William Jarman won approval to operate a turnpike on the road between Brown's Gap and the commercial center at Mechums River; by providing some permanent surfacing and maintaining the roadway that they had begun improving in 1790, they were permitted to collect tolls for its use. It was the first turnpike in Albemarle.

In the 1930s, when the Blue Ridge Mountains became a national park, the roads into the mountains were closed off at the ridge, much to the anguish of tradesmen and displaced families who had made the mountains home for two centuries. Some still spoke in dialects of early settlers.

To build the Blue Ridge Parkway and Skyline Drive, the federal government martialed the Civilian Conservation Corps, men ages 18 to 20 made jobless by the Depression. Beginning in 1935, the C.C.C. established four camps along the route; one was near Boonesville.

Ninety per cent of the workers were drawn from the area in which they worked. The men earned $30 per month and sent $12 to their families. The farms they came from earned an average of only $86 per year in the late 1920s; even so, they had been self-sustaining.

Cross the river to see an adjacent Brown home, **Brightberry.**

Return to SR 810 (which is called the Browns Gap Turnpike south of this junction) and continue southward through the **Brown's Cove** community.

The picturesque Doyles River rolls along beside the road. **Branch Point,** marked by a gate on the left, was another of the Brown family farms. It dates from 1780.

The community of Brown's Cove stretches almost a mile to the south. One of the most isolated of Albemarle's communities, Brown's Cove still retains the essence of mountaineering independence. Feuding, in the tradition of the Hatfields and the McCoys, is not unknown here.

At one end of the community is the **Schifflett Grocery** and at the other is the **Morris Grocery;** between them is the **Mount Carmel Baptist Church,** on the right. Across the road from the church is a house with an old school building in the yard.

About two tenths of a mile south of the Morris Grocery, look for Walnut Level Road (SR 668). Turn right and drive about a mile and a half.

On the left is **Walnut Level,** the principal home of patriarch Benjamin Brown, Sr., built around 1800.

Innisfree, an intentional community, is dedicated to helping the handicapped individuals who reside here with independence in group cottages. The residents create some fine hand-woven items, sold at area craft fairs.

Backtrack to Browns Gap Turnpike and continue south. In three tenths of a mile, turn right onto Slam Gate Road (SR 673) to see **Montfair,** the site of the first Brown family home. Go past the house and turn around at the campground entrance. The house is better seen on your return to the turnpike.

The original Montfair, the center of the Doylesville community, was destroyed by fire in 1846. This house was built in 1848. Colonel William Brown hired carpenters who had worked on the University of Virginia to create the house's woodwork. Buildings that served as a school and a store still stand.

The ghost of an unknown woman has reportedly been seen many times over the years. The most recent was in the 1960s, when a visitor who knew nothing of the ghost stories awakened in the night and saw a lady dressed in black at the end of her bed.

Jubal Early, who married a daughter of this family, suffered a wound in the last battle of the Civil War fought west of the Blue Ridge, at Waynesboro. According to family lore, the general was unable to dismount his horse, so rode the long distance to Montfair without respite. He parted company with his horse only after riding it right up the steps and onto the front porch.

About three miles south of Montfair the turnpike crosses **Moormans River** (named for Thomas Moorman, a Quaker prominent in the early days).

In another half mile the Brown's Gap Turnpike makes a 90-degree turn to the left at the junction with Sugar Hollow Road (SR 614). This is the village of **White Hall.**

White Hall was an election precinct early on in the county's history. It has had many names through the years: Glenn's Store, William Maupin's Store, Maupin's Tavern, Miller's Tavern and Shumate's Tavern. The present name was adopted about 1835.

Garrison's Store stands on the corner. Inside is the local post office in an old cage, well worth a peek. Look behind the modern store to see the much older one, now used for storage.

During World War II, a prison of war camp was located in the field north of the store. In August 1944, 260 German prisoners, part of Rommel's crack North African Corps, were held here. These prisoners filled a labor shortage during a year of bumper crops in the orchards in the Crozet-White Hall region.

During the war years, apple production increased 50% and peach production 100%; women and children also harvested the fruit.

East of the junction is **Wyant's Store,** one of the oldest in the country. In operation from 1888, it was rebuilt in 1935.

Before you leave White Hall: five miles to the west on Sugar Hollow Road, in Sugar Hollow itself, is one of the largest reservoirs in Albemarle County, stocked with mountain trout in the spring. The road to Sugar Hollow (named for the maples found there) is a beautiful forested drive that crisscrosses Moormans River as it tumbles down the Blue Ridge.

This tour ends here.

To return to Charlottesville by the most direct route, continue on the Browns Gap Turnpike (right at Wyant's Store, then left at the top of the rise where the Browns Gap Turnpike follows SR 680) to Mechums River. From there take the Three Notched Road (US 250) east.

[Note: Tour 6 begins here, at Wyant's Store.]

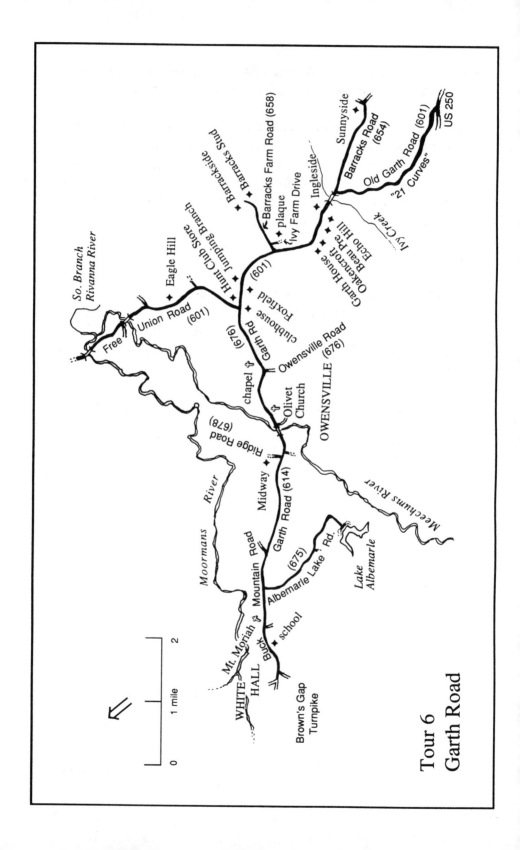

Tour 6
Garth Road

Tour 6   Garth Road

From White Hall to Charlottesville: 9 miles

Garth Road finds its history in 19th-century horse farms, fox-and-hounds, steeplechase racing and patrician riding academies, though British and Hessian prisoners of war found it less genteel in Revolutionary times.

[This is the final leg of three tours that may be combined into a loop: Tours 4, 5 and 6.]

To reach White Hall from the Visitors Center, take I-64 west to exit 107. Follow the Rockfish Gap Turnpike (US 250) east about a mile and a half and turn left onto Crozet Avenue (VA 240 and SR 810). In about five miles you will reach the junction with Buck Mountain road (SR 614) in the little community of **White Hall** (described on page 60). Turn right (east) to begin this tour.

Buck Mountain Road passes the abandoned **White Hall School,** on the right, just before you reach **Mount Moriah Church,** on the left. Behind the church is **Maupin's Orchard.**

> Mount Moriah began as Maupin's Meeting House in 1788. The first church was constructed in 1834 and enlarged in 1854. Mount Moriah's work in evangelizing slaves was ambitious, and this Methodist congregation absorbed many Quakers at the advent of the Revolution.

Lake Albemarle, a part of the county reservoir system, is popular among bass fishermen. To get there, turn right on Albemarle Lake Road (SR 675).

About a half mile past the road to the lake, go straight through the junction to get onto Garth Road (still SR 614). Buck Mountain Road turns left (on SR 671).

In another mile you will pass the sign for **Midway,** a Garth family home that took its name from its location, midway between White Hall and Charlottesville. To see the house, turn left on Ridge Road (SR 678) and go about three tenths of a mile.

> This federal-style country brick has charming oddities, like a window too close to a pillar and a door that is off center, the result of a building process begun about 1760.
>
> In 1860, as the family grew and prospered, a second house was added beside the original. Later the two houses were connected and a columned porch was put across the front to tie all the parts together.
>
> The Garths, who owned thousands of acres in this section of the county, were enthusiastic horse people. In the mid 19th century they founded Garth's Fox Hunt Club and a race track on nearby Ivy Creek. Garth descendants continued breeding and racing horses in this area into the mid 20th century.

Return to Garth Road and turn left. About a mile and a half from Midway is the 1880 **Olivet Presbyterian Church,** which marks the remnants of **Owensville.**

SR 614 ends here and Garth Road now follows SR 676 (south of the junction SR 676 is called the Owensville Road). Just past the junction, on the left, is a tiny, picturesque private chapel.

> William Faulkner owned a farm about a mile into the woods to the southeast (the right side of the road), when he was writer-in-residence at the University of Virginia 1958-1962. Faulkner, who loved to ride, was a member of the Farming-

ton Hunt, which owned the land between his farm and this road.

Faulkner spent his time in Albemarle trying to master his horse. He preferred the company of trainers and grooms to the literati, and only aped the country gentlemen when the hunt met.

In about a mile, at the Hunt Country Corner store, turn left onto Free Union Road (SR 601), for a scenic side trip.

About a mile and a half from the turn, **Eagle Hill,** an elegant tribute to South Carolina coastal architecture, crowns a hill on the right.

The road crosses the Mechums and Moormans rivers, here about a mile apart. Both carry the Virginia Scenic River designation. They meet to the east to form the south branch of the Rivanna River. This is a put-in point for canoeists.

Turn around when it is safe to do so, and return to Garth Road. Turn left to the **Hunt Country Corner** store.

Once known as Woodson's store, it was called Vandevender's Store for much of this century for its owner, George Vandevender, the long-time Huntsman of the Farmington Hunt and the owner of Foxfield Farm.

The building opposite the store was once the **Farmington Hunt clubhouse,** where Faulkner joined with other members for some famous parties.

In two tenths of a mile, on the right, a recycled airplane hangar signals **Foxfield,** a steeplechase course created in 1976 on Vandevender's farm as a memorial to him.

Foxfield attracts thousands of spectators to its two national steeplechase meetings each year in spring and fall.

In 1929, before Vandevender owned the farm, the Dixie Flying Service operated an airport and flying school here. Wood Field was named in honor of Robert "Buck" Wood, a local aviator who died in France in 1918. The famous aviator Billy Mitchell officially opened of the field. Within two years the small flying service had transported 1,052 passengers, but that wasn't enough to save the fledgling company from the dead calm of the Depression.

Jumping Branch, opposite Foxfield, was designed by restoration architect Milton Grigg, an Albemarle resident whose work in Virginia in the 1940s and 50s earned him a favorable reputation for outstanding rejuvenations or adaptations of 18th-century houses.

About a mile and a half past Foxfield, turn left on Barracks Farm Road (SR 658) to the **Barracks Stud** riding academy for a view of what was once a large Revolutionary prisoner of war campground called The Barracks. Not a trace remains, but we have good historical accounts of what it was like.

Colonel John Harvie, who lived at Belmont on the Fredericksburg Road, used his political clout to win the contract for housing the English and Hessian prisoners taken by the Americans after the victory at Saratoga in October 1777.

The prisoners were at first quartered in Massachusetts, where food was scarce and the winter long. In October, 1778, Congress decided to move them to Virginia.

It took the 4,000 prisoners 70 days to march 628 miles through an unusually severe winter. They reached Albemarle in January 1779 and found the famous Charlottesville to consist only of a courthouse, a tavern and a dozen houses. The prisoners far outnumbered the local population; their camp was for a time one of the bigger towns in Virginia.

When they arrived, the prison camp offered only roofless huts for their lodging. Far worse, the provisions for the prisoners had not arrived, forcing them to subsist on corn cakes for six days.

The officers fared better. Major General William Phillips, the British commander, was housed at Blenheim; the German commander at Colle, near Monticello.

In time things improved somewhat, and some of the more literary of them organized a theater with three sets of scenery and a curtain bearing a harlequin. Not surprisingly, their comedies satirized Americans.

Although they cultivated small gardens and apparently had some freedom to move about, conditions declined again and by the fall of 1780, when only 2,100 prisoners remained, there were reports of enormous rats and insect-riddled log houses. It wasn't Andersonville, but it wasn't a month in the country, either.

The brick house, **Barrackside,** backed up to the mountains, was built in 1819 by Garland Garth, who bought the land from the Harvie family.

Backtrack on Barracks Farm Road and turn left on Ivy Farm Drive. In half a mile, just past Stillhouse Road, there is a contemporary brick house, on the left.

Near the road is a **plaque** commemorating some Revolutionary prisoners of war whose graves were discovered when the house was built.

Return to Garth Road and turn left. In a half a mile, on the right, is the **Garth House** (1780).

> This house is identified with the early generations of the Garth family who owned all the land on both sides of Garth Road for many miles in both directions.

Beyond the house, on the right, is the **Oakencroft Vineyard,** where you may see wine making in season and sample recent prize-winning vintages.

Another Garth holding, **Ingleside,** on the left, is identified by the three cupolas on each of its huge stables.

> This was the track and horse breeding farm begun by William Garth. Bertha Garth Jones, who owned and operated the stables and taught riding in this century, was Master of the Farmington Hunt.

Just past Ingleside, down a hill and across **Ivy Creek,** is the junction with Barracks Road (SR 654). Go straight on Barracks Road a mile to see the former home of Confederate colonel R.T.W. Duke. After the entrance to Colthurst (easy to see on the right), look for large white house on the hill to the left.

> General Sheridan's men rode to Duke's house, then called **Sunnyside,** from the Ivy Road in an unsuccessful search for the colonel of the 46th Virginia Regiment. Duke, who purchased the house in May 1863, was a member of Virginia's House of Delegates, three times the commonwealth's attorney and a U.S. congressman.

Turn around at the Montvue sign or another convenient place. Go back to the junction at Ivy Creek and turn left on Old Garth Road (SR 601).

This two mile stretch of road is dubbed **Twenty-one Curves** by the local folks for a very good reason.

Turn right at the stop sign to reach US 250, the 250 Bypass and I-64. The tour ends here.

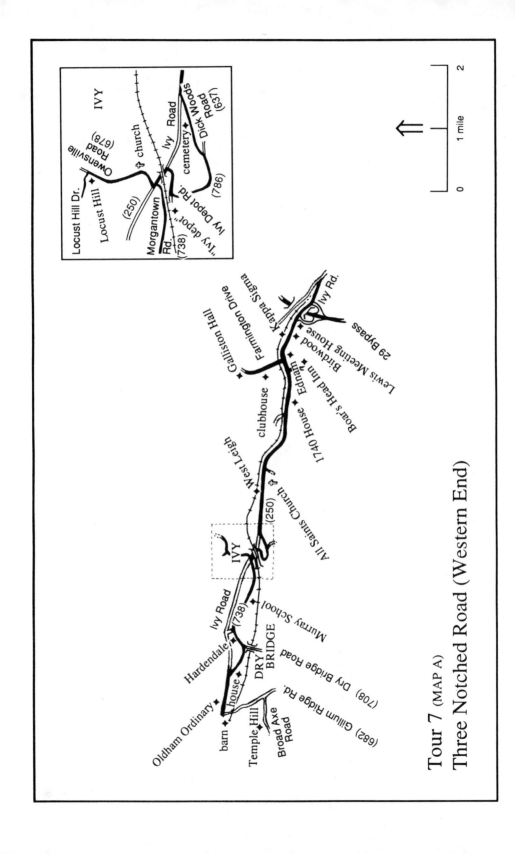

Tour 7 (MAP A)
Three Notched Road (Western End)

Tour 7   Three Notched Road (Western End)

From Charlottesville, through Ivy and Crozet,
to Jarman's Gap: 18 miles

Most of the historic roads pushed into Albemarle from the east, including the eastern end of Three Notched Road. The section just west of Charlottesville, however, was a west-to-east project. The Shenandoah Valley culture influenced this part of the county, and the railroad sparked the development of three major depot towns, Ivy, Mechums River and Crozet.

From the Visitors Center, go west on I-64 to the US 29 bypass north (Exit 118B). Take the second exit, US 250 west.

Spreading out from this intersection was the plantation of David Lewis, who patented land here in the 1730s. Just opposite the Piedmont Tractor company is the **site** of the 1781 **Lewis Meeting House,** the first Baptist church in the area.

> Western Albemarle was settled by dissenters: Presbyterians, Baptists and a few Quakers. Although Anglican ministers complained of the separatists as early as 17151, the Baptists did not erect churches here until 30 years later, when this meeting house was built. Their numbers swelled in the last 1700s, following the disestablishment of the Anglican as the state church at the Revolution. By 1869 there were 50 clergymen in Albemarle, and half were Baptists.

Just past the church site, where there is a left turn lane, turn left into the grounds of the **Birdwood Pavilion,** a guest house of the University of Virginia surrounded by a golf course.

Elegant Birdwood still keeps its various dependencies and romantic, free-standing brick observation tower. William Garth, grandson of the great landowner Thomas Garth, built it all in 1818, on land first patented by Lewis.

Return to Ivy Road and turn left. **Kappa Sigma** fraternity's national headquarters is directly opposite the Birdwood entrance.

The **Institute of Textile Technology,** adjacent to Kappa Sigma, occupies the **Boxwood** estate.

Owned at the end of the 19th century by the family of businessman, banker and developer Hollis P. Rinehart, the gracious home serves as a training school for textile manufacturing managers, a sort of mini graduate school for updating industry knowledge.

Turn left at the traffic signal and bear left up the hill to see **Ednam,** a sturdy dowager of an old home now the centerpiece of a condominium development.

The house was designed in 1905 by Richmond architect D. Wiley Anderson for Edwin O. Meyer, a New York importer. It is a Virginia Historic Landmark.

Back at the traffic signal, cross the railroad tracks into **Farmington,** a *creme de la creme* 1930s country club community. The clubhouse, ahead on the left, was designed by Thomas Jefferson.

Francis Jerdone, a notable Tory at the beginning of the Revolution, began the house before 1780. The new American government seized his 3,000 acres, but somehow Jerdone reacquired it and sold it to George Divers in 1785. Jefferson and Divers competed annually to see who could bring green peas to the table first; winner fed peas to loser.

The building has been enlarged considerably since it was completed in 1802, but the facade remains much as Jefferson designed it, although he was distressed to find that the workmen had botched the proportions of the columns on the portico. In 1927 the house and its remaining 350 acres became the Farmington Country Club.

Continue on Farmington Drive a mile past the clubhouse to glimpse **Galliston Hall,** a Virginia Historic Landmark, through its regal iron gate.

Built in 1931-32, it incorporates elements from colonial Virginia plantation houses as well as the Governor's Palace in Williamsburg. The design of the doorway was borrowed from Westover, on the James River, and the cluster of chimneys is modeled on the 17th-century Bacon's Castle. In 1990 it was featured in the Hollywood film, "True Colors."

Return to Ivy Road and turn right. Turn left almost immediately to the **Boar's Head Inn,** owned by the University of Virginia.

The right wing of the central building incorporates the 1837 Martin Dawson mill, moved here from Red Hill. It is post-and-beam construction, with magnificent hickory-pegged heartwood pine beams twelve to fourteen inches thick.

Return to Ivy Road and continue a mile and a half west to the **1740 House,** a Virginia Historic Landmark that is also on the national historic registry, on the left.

This building stands at the beginning of the west-to-east section of the Three Notched Road: milepost 0. The road was later improved westward from here to the Valley of Virginia.

Originally known as the D.S. Tavern, the establishment took its name from a tree carved with the letters D.S. The initials may have been those of David Stockton, the man credited with cutting the road. It is more likely, however, that they stood for dissenter, a marking found elsewhere in Virginia.

Continue westward about a mile. On the left is the **All Saints Anglican Church** (1989), which still uses the traditional Book of Common Prayer. **West Leigh,** on the right, is a magnificent Greek Revival brick mansion, the most impressive in the Ivy area.

In about a half mile get into the left lane and turn onto Dick Woods Road (SR 637) to follow the original path of the Three Notched Road. Almost immediately, on the right, is a cemetery that contains some Confederate graves.

Bear right onto Ivy Depot Road (SR 786). As you approach the one-lane bridge, look right to see the stone foundations of a mill. Cross Ivy Creek and pass by the miller's cottage, also on the right. Turn right into **Ivy.**

> The village, known first as Woodville, became Ivy in the mid 9th century when the railroad named its depot Ivy Station for the bushy *kalmia,* an ivy-like plant that grew profusely along the creek banks.

Turn left and go under the railroad bridge. Turn right onto the Owensville Road (SR 678) for a brief detour from the Three Notched Road.

On the hillside to the right, just above the turn, bear right to see **St. Paul's Ivy,** an Episcopal church that began as a mission near Mechum's River around 1836-38. In its graveyard are a variety of graceful tombstones with names linked to the history of the area.

> Frederick William Neve, the British-born rector of this church from 1888 to 1923, rode his horse into the coves and hollows of the Blue Ridge and Ragged Mountains to establish

chapels and schools. He personified the missionary zeal that was the hallmark of religious groups here at the turn of the century. He enlisted his wealthy neighbors in the work of improving the lives of those who lived in impoverished isolation, including Nancy Langhorne, who would one day become Lady Astor. Neve founded the Blue Ridge School at Dyke and even tried to establish a college for women at Ivy when a move was afoot to make the then all-male University of Virginia accept female students.

Half a mile north on the Owensville Road, on the left, is **Locust Hill,** the birthplace of Meriwether Lewis and now a private residence. Go past the entrance and turn left on Locust Hill Drive (SR 1608) to get a better look.

The main clapboard house incorporates a log cabin that dates to the 1740s, thought to be the original home. In 1740 Robert Lewis patented land on Ivy Creek which was eventually inherited by Meriwether's mother, Lucy Marks. Meriwether was born here in 1744; the place became his when he was 21.

In the 1770s some British prisoners of war, apparently free to travel the countryside from their Barracks prison only a few miles north, visited Locust Hill and grew rowdy. Lucy, whose husband was off fighting for independence, pulled the musket from her wall and ordered them from her property. So handy with a gun was she, that while the menfolk were hunting one day she shot a deer in her yard and presented it, nicely roasted, to the unsuccessful hunters on their return.

Meriwether farmed Locust Hill briefly but soon left to lead a 4,000-mile expedition for his mentor, Thomas Jefferson. Lewis and William Clark, another son of Albemarle, explored the Louisiana Purchase in 1802-03 and opened the territory that more than doubled the size of the United States.

Return now to Ivy. Turn left on Ivy Road, then make a quick right turn on Morgantown Road (SR 738), named for a village that once stood about a mile from here. You are, once again, following the path of the original Three Notched Road.

On the left, look for a two-story brick store, now a private home, that local residents call the Ivy depot, although the vanished stone depot was farther down the track. This building was, in fact, the **Ivy General Store.** The walking bridge across the tracks marks the site of a carriageway that once linked two sections of the road.

The houses on the left side for the next mile constitute what remains of rural Ivy. This black community's origins reach back to the decades following the Civil War.

The **Murray School,** on the left, was built as a black school following the Brown vs. Board of Education ruling, in response to what was an obvious inequity between the black school then in use and the school serving white students. It now serves black and white, and was recently enlarged.

About a mile past the school, on the right, is the columned **Hardendale** manor house.

This farm first belonged to Michael Woods, leader of a party of about thirty Scotch-Irish immigrants who entered Albemarle from the west in the early 1730s and dominated settlement in this area. Woods himself acquired 3,300 acres between Mechums River and Ivy. In 1737 Woods cleared a road between the Blue Ridge and Ivy Creek, thus extending the Three Notched Road west of milepost 0.

Benjamin Hardin, a later owner, built a large public house here in 1826 and called it the Hotel Albemarle. He kept a stable of race horses and had a fine barn in front of the tavern.

West of Hardendale is the junction with Dry Bridge Road (SR 708), named for **Dry Bridge,** a very old black community that took its name from a bridge over the railroad track.

Bear right to continue west on Morgantown Road. Where the road bends north, look for a cottage-style house behind a split rail fence, on the left. This was the home of Richard Wood, for whom Woodville (now Ivy) was named.

> The house, originally a Greek Revival design with a full second story, dates to the 1850s, when Ivy experienced the growth and prosperity that arrived with the railroad. A fire destroyed the upper floor, and the house was remodelled in this 1920s cottage style, a radical transformation.

Turn left onto US 250, which here is called the Rockfish Gap Turnpike. Be extremely careful at this blind junction.

The **James Oldham Ordinary** sits in the grove of trees on the rise behind the red barn on the right. The original roadbed followed Oldham's driveway.

> In the early days, the ford just west of here was the only convenient crossing of the Mechums River. Oldham, a contractor for some of the buildings at the University of Virginia, purchased this property from Benjamin Hardin in 1828. He died in 1843, before the railroad arrived, but still saw enough travelers to keep his ordinary thriving.

The **Crafter's Gallery,** at the junction with Gillum Ridge Road (SR 682), was once James Oldham's barn.

The Kinsolving plantation, **Temple Hill,** which is totally hidden when there are leaves on the trees, is about a mile and a half down Gillum Ridge Road. To get there, follow Gillum Ridge, then turn right on Broad Axe Road (a continuation of SR 682).

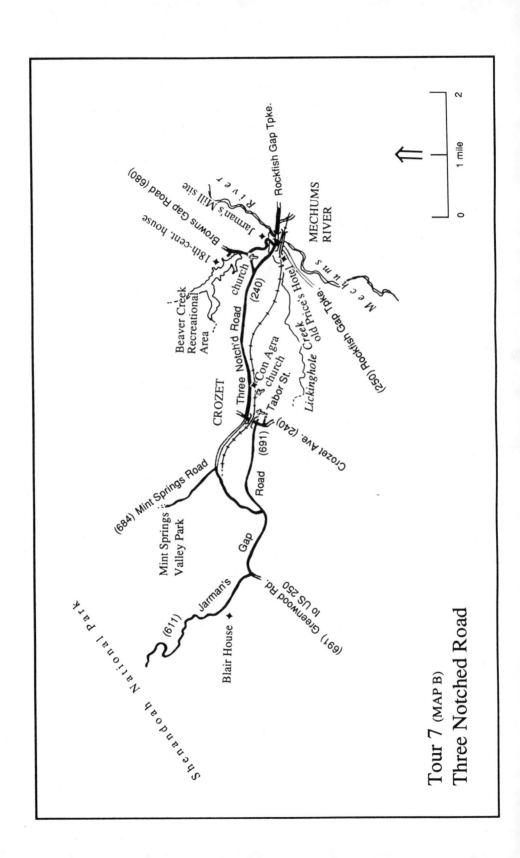

Tour 7 (MAP B)
Three Notched Road

Between 1788 and his death in 1829, James Kinsolving acquired 1,400 acres on both sides of Mechums River; he built his home on Broad Axe Creek. The Kinsolvings were vestrymen and ministers of the Episcopal church at North Garden; one descendant became the bishop of Brazil and another the bishop of west Texas.

Continue on (or return to) the Rockfish Gap Turnpike. Bear right immediately after crossing the river (don't go under the bridge) and stop here to learn about the **Mechums River** community.

The ford across this river, named for an early settler, was one of the principle gateways of westward expansion in the 18th and 19th centuries. Here was the crossroads of the Three Notched Road, the Rockfish Gap Turnpike, the Brown's Gap Turnpike and Broad Axe Road.

In 1837, when the Louisa Railroad Company wanted to connect the Great Valley of Virginia with the Tidewater, state engineer Claudius Crozet identified Rockfish Gap (southwest of here) as the best crossing through the mountains. The tiny commercial center of Mechums River, lying directly on the railroad route, was destined for boom times.

Wooden wagon bridges had already replaced the ford. There was a public ice house, post office and tanyard. A bark mill adjoined the smithy. And then the railroad arrived.

This became the staging area for a four-year project (1848-52) that was budgeted at $300,000. The seventeen miles from Mechums River to Waynesboro were the most expensive, requiring three miles of mountain tunneling in three sections.

At the western end of the railroad bridge is a private home that was once **Price's Hotel,** built next to the depot. It is best seen in winter.

Its exact date is unclear, but newspapers from the summer of 1857 were found stuffed in a wall during restoration. Charles H. Price bought the building and 192 acres in 1872 from the heirs of John Mosby, a relative of the Confederate raider, but it was probably William Graves (who owned it in 1848) who built the original hotel.

The hotel served commercial travelers and vacationers who enjoyed this scenic spot where the river cut though high hills from north to south and animals sought the natural salts exposed on the banks of Lickinghole Creek. Even into the 1920s, the hotel centered an active community with a tomato cannery, a water-powered flour mill, two stores, a school and a sand quarry.

Turn onto Browns Gap Road (SR 680) and follow the signs for Beaver Creek Park. The site of **Jarman's Mill,** at the junction of creek and river, is across the bridge, on the right.

Some of the 18th-century stonework can be seen near the road. The well-preserved miller's house is on the hillside around the curve. William Jarman's gristmill was an impressive four-story structure with a long mill race.

The miller's house is ahead on the right. Drive on toward the park.

About 1790 Jarman and his partner, Benjamin Brown, began to improve this section of the original Three Notched Road.

In 1862, a traveler might have met a ragged line of 16,000 Confederate soldiers heading south. After several quick raids on the Union forces, Stonewall Jackson and his men disappeared from the Valley of Virginia by crossing the mountains at Brown's Gap. They marched down this turnpike in the rain and camped overnight in the hills around Mechums River; legend has it that Jackson himself slept in Price's Hotel.

On Monday, May 4, the troops left here by train for McDowell, a village west of Staunton, where the Union army thought it impossible for them to be. This tactic had far-reaching consequences, as it prevented Union generals Irvin McDowell and George B. McClellan from joining forces for an attack on General Robert E. Lee's Confederate army near Richmond.

Continue another half mile to the **Mountain Plains Church.**

The church took its name from Mountain Plains, a plantation that was part of the original Michael Woods grant. Presbyterianism was hugely successful in winning converts from the established Anglican church in the years before the Revolution; the first meeting house was built here in the 1740s.

Mountain Plains became a Baptist church in 1882. In September 1959 a tornado damaged the front of the church, which was rebuilt.

A tenth of a mile beyond the church is the **Beaver Creek Recreational Area,** part of the county reservoir system. It is open for fishing and boating. Cross the **dam** and turn left into the park.

The dam is named for Charles Mercer Garnett, Sr., who was responsible for Albemarle having the first county executive form of government in the United States.

From the farthest parking lot you may be able to see, across a narrow finger of the lake, an abandoned 18th-century house.

One of the oldest in the area, it was the home of William Woods, who went to Philadelphia in 1751 to plead for a preacher from the Presbyterian synod.

Retrace your path and turn right on Three Notch'd Road (SR 802) at Mountain Plains church. In just under half a mile, at the **Mount**

Salem Baptist Church (1893), turn right onto Three Notch'd Road (now following VA 240), part of the original roadway. It is about two and a half miles to **Crozet.**

On the way you'll pass several farms dating from the late 19th and early 20th centuries and the **Conagra Frozen Foods** plant, which was originally a fruit cannery.

Across the tracks, just past Conagra, was the first public black school in the county (1916), now vanished. It stood beside the **Union Baptist Church** (1914), built by a black congregation and still in use.

In Crozet, turn left at the stop sign, go under the railroad bridge and turn left again to park in front of the quaint Main Street stores.

A depot, subscribed for by local residents and named for Claudius Crozet, opened in 1877 to serve the growing orchard industry and the Miller School. The six miles of road between the depot and school were macadamized, the first hard-surfaced road in the county. Crozet was positioned for growth. The 1890s saw the establishment of a bank, an elementary school, churches and at least a dozen small businesses.

The local soil, a nutritive Cecil clay, is ideal for growing fruit. By the mid-1920s, the annual production of 60 orchards had reached 150,000 barrels of apples and 500,000 crates of peaches. Over 500,000 fruit trees were set out between 1925 and 1935. Crozet led the state in the production of Albemarle pippins and winesap apples. One distributor dispatched nearly three dozen railroad car loads of peaches in one day in the 1930s.

A new brick depot was built in 1923; it became the Crozet Library in 1983. The Crozet Cold Storage Plant, the tallest building in Crozet, once held 65,000 barrels of fruit; today it is a residential facility for senior citizens.

The old Three Notched Road ran on this side of the depot rather than north of it, as the road does today.

Turn left onto Crozet Avenue (VA 240), pass the old and new Crozet Methodist church buildings, and turn left on Tabor Street a short block to see the picturesque **Tabor Presbyterian Church.**

This congregation evolved from the Lebanon Presbyterian Church and dates to 1833. It moved here from Brownsville to serve the expanded population following the coming of the railroad in the 1850s.

Backtrack to Crozet Avenue, turn right and then left onto Jarman's Gap Road (SR 691) to follow the path of the old Three Notched Road.

In a mile and a half turn right on Mint Springs Road (SR 684) for a side trip to **Mint Springs Valley Park,** with its lake in a mountain cove. At the stop sign in a mile, turn left for eight tenths of a mile.

The park was once part of the Wayland Orchard, the first commercial orchard in this area in the 1890s. (There is an entrance fee to the park, and swimming is permitted.)

Backtrack to Jarmans Gap Road and turn right.

This road passes through the heart of active orchard country with mountains rising immediately on the right and the flat plain of Lickinghole Creek and Mechums River with all their small tributary creeks spreading southward.

In a mile and a tenth, bear right to follow Jarmans Gap Road (now SR 611) to its dead end near **Jarman's Gap,** about three miles.

[Note: This steep, narrow road is intermittently paved, but can be negotiated without a four-wheel-drive vehicle. Be careful not to overheat your brakes on the way down.]

> This gap, then called Woods Gap, was used by the first settlers who crossed the Blue Ridge from the Shenandoah Valley to claim virgin land here in the 1730s. This tortuous mountain road was abandoned when the Rockfish Gap Turnpike was completed in the late 1820s. Many highly independent mountain men and women lived in the hollows of this unaltered landscape—and some still do.

In the 1800s this area was known as **Blair Park** for the plantation of John Blair, justice of the U.S. Supreme Court (1789-96), about a mile from the turn.

> Orchardist Walter Minsing replaced the original house in the 1920s. Glimpse his stone chateau. His orchards lay at his feet.

State maintenance of the road ends in another 2.1 mile, near the edge of the **Shenandoah National Park,** the western boundary of the county. The road comes within a half mile of the Appalachian Trail, but this is not a recommended access point.

To return to Charlottesville, backtrack and turn right (south) on Greenwood Road (SR 691). It will take you to US 250 (2.6 miles). Turn left to reach I-64, about two miles to the east.

Tour 8   Rockfish Gap Turnpike

From Mechums River to Greenwood to
Rockfish Gap: 11 miles

In 1826 the Charlottesville merchants pressured the Virginia legislature to improve the roads from Charlottesville to the Valley in
an effort to salvage some of the trade that had begun to bypass the
city on the newly-opened Staunton-James River Turnpike, which
linked the Valley directly to the wharves at Scottsville. The result-
ing Rockfish Gap Turnpike incorporated the Three Notched Road
from Charlottesville to the Mechums River, then turned southwest
to meet the Staunton Road at Afton Mountain—very nearly the
route followed by US 250 today.

From the Visitors Center, turn left at the traffic signal to I-64 west.
Exit I-64 US 29 bypass north (Exit 118B) and take US 250 to
Mechums River, about eight miles in all.

[Note: the sights along US 250 from the bypass to Mechums River
are described in Tour 7.]

Mechums River is one of the lost towns of Albemarle, established at a convenient ford where Lickinghole Creek enters the
river. The Monacans, also drawn by the ford, established a camp-
site on the west bank of the river long before the European settlers
arrived.

[A detailed description of the old town of Mechums River may be
found in Tour 7, pages 79 to 80.]

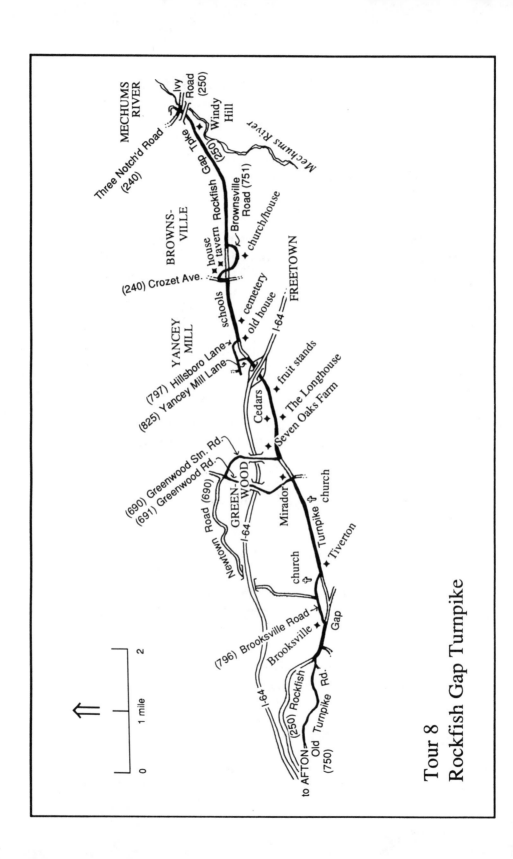

Tour 8
Rockfish Gap Turnpike

Follow the Rockfish Gap Turnpike (US 250) west as it curves left under the railroad bridge. Beyond the bridge, look right to see the few buildings that remain of the village.

A half mile past the bridge is the entrance to **Windyhill,** a home above you, on the left.

> The driveway is part of the old roadbed of this turnpike, which ran along Windyhill's high ridge and then swung west, across the present road, to a ridge on the right. One of Windyhill's outbuildings is the old block post office.

In half a mile, note the ridge behind the cluster of stores on the right; the old road followed the ridge. You can see its path for about three tenths of a mile, to where it curves back across today's road and follows what is now Brownsville Road.

Turn left onto Brownsville Road (SR 751, gravel for a tenth of a mile), then bear right.

Continue three tenths of a mile to the one-and-half-story clapboard house on the left which was once the **Tabor Presbyterian Church,** built about 1853, and is now a private home.

> When the railroad arrived in 1852-53, the population around Brownsville merited a church of its own. The Lebanon Presbyterian Church (west about three miles) had a preaching station at Brownsville that grew into this church, used until the congregation moved into the more populous Crozet. Thomas Black, the grandson of the first minister called to the first Presbyterian church in Albemarle—Mountain Plains at Mechums River—gave the land.

This roads curves back to Rockfish Gap Turnpike. Turn left at the stop sign, and then turn right almost immediately on Brownsville Road. This is the center of **Brownsville.**

At the turn, on the right, you will see (especially in winter when the trees are bare) a long clapboard building sitting at a diagonal to the road. Local lore tells us this was a tavern built in the early 19th century.

There were at least five inns, taverns or roadhouses in the scant ten miles between Mechums River and the foot of the Blue Ridge Mountains, showing how needful were the drovers and travelers for lodging and food.

Around the curve, take a good look at the brick house on the right; it has two entrances.

This house is made up of three structures. One was built about 1818-20 by Francis Browning. Another was added by John Dettor, Jr., around 1833. An even earlier frame house was moved to the rear of the brick sections. The second entrance may have accommodated a shop or business or quarters for another family, perhaps another generation.

To return to the highway, turn left at the stop sign on Crozet Avenue (VA 240) and then right at the blinking traffic signal.

Modern Brownsville is an educational center with three county schools. Western Albemarle High School was built in the 1970s. On the right are the Brownsville Elementary and the J.T. Henley Middle School, named for a local orchardist.

The **Hillsboro Cemetery** (on the left, just past the high school) has some lovely tombstones that date from the mid 19th century. The Brownsville Market is next on the left and beyond it are remnants of a black community called **Freetown.**

At the junction with Hillsboro Lane (SR 797) pull onto the shoulder to look across at one of the original Freetown homes, now over a hundred years old.

Turn right on Hillsboro Lane. Here the turnpike passed through a village once called Hillsboro and now known as **Yancey Mill.**

To view Yancey Mill is like parting a curtain into the 19th century. It is a typically compact rural village; residences, shops, church and VFW hall stand cheek-by-jowl. The terrain behind the row of houses on the right drops off to reveal grazing land, and beyond is a dramatic mountain vista typical of western Albemarle.

On the left is a board and batten house (wide vertical boards with narrow laths sealing the joints) with a long front porch and tin roof, once the general merchandise store; earlier in this century it was a restaurant called the Green Teapot. The Wiley family, well-known orchardists, lived in the two houses opposite.

The left end of the **Hillsboro Baptist Church** is the original, built about 1850 in Gothic Revival style.

The **VFW Hall** (1862) stands opposite the church. T.C. Bowen, a teacher who operated a school near here in the 1860s, gave the land to the Sons of Temperance under the condition that they build a meeting hall. Apparently the temperance movement failed, because Bowen again donated the lot, this time with "town hall," to a Freemasons lodge in 1869. Today it houses the local chapter of the Veterans of Foreign Wars.

It is easy to evoke the pleasures of a rural community by studying these buildings—one where small treats, like new sewing needles or a chaw of tobacco could be obtained; another where a pot-luck dinner and program might be enjoyed; and the third where refuge from the vagaries of life could be sought.

The shingle-sided house just west of the VFW Hall and the clapboard house opposite it were built before 1850. The shingles cover a log house. The clapboard house has been a Yancey family home since 1862.

The Yanceys, who arrived in the county in 1765, established a saw mill south of town in the mid 19th century; it is still in the family. The business was so important to the town, that the town itself became known as Yancey Mill when it was discovered that Virginia had another town called Hillsboro.

The long board-and-batten building on the left, near the end of the town, was called the Dutch Garden in the 1920s. It was a popular restaurant and meeting place run by a 6'8" Dutchman named Baissevanis.

Turn around at the dead end sign, then turn right onto Yancey Mill Lane (SR 825) at the shingle-sided house to return to the highway. Turn right again.

In seven tenths of a mile past the I-64 interchange, on the left, are two fruit stands, **Morris's** and **Maupin's,** where local peaches, apples and other produce are available in season.

Two tenths of a mile past the fruit stands are **The Cedars,** on the right, and **The Longhouse** (opposite). Both are on property once owned by Charles Yancey.

The Cedars, a Virginia Historic Landmark, was built in the ten years preceding the Civil War by Col. John S. Cocke, who ran a tavern on the lower floor. One wonders why Cocke build such a magnificent edifice in the Greek Revival style; one possible explanation is that it was also his home. At any rate, he eventually lost his tavern home in settling gambling debts. During the Civil War, The Cedars may have been used as a hospital. Later it was a school for boys.

Chiswell Langhorne, a self-made railroad tycoon, and his gaming friends turned the tavern into a real gambling hall called The Casino during the Gay Nineties.

The Longhouse served as a dormitory when The Cedars was a school. In the late 18th century it was a tavern owned by Charles Yancey, who also had a store, mill and distillery here. It was for a while known as **May's Tavern** for a later owner, Elijah May. Today it backs up to the Yogi Bear Campground.

Seven Oaks Farm is across the road from the campground. In the late spring there is a pick-your-own strawberry patch here, and in the fall a pick-your-own pumpkin patch.

Once called Clover Plains, the 1848 house is both a Virginia and National Historic Landmark. Neither it nor Black's Tavern (1796) can be seen from the road.

George Rogers Clark stopped at Black's Tavern on his journey when he sought Governor Patrick Henry's assistance in obtaining back pay for his soldiers following the victory at Vincennes.

Two tenths of a mile past Seven Oaks, turn right on Newtown Road (SR 690) and go one mile to visit **Greenwood,** a small rural community that grew up around a railway depot and is now known for its annual arts and crafts fairs.

The little depot was visited by General Sheridan, who blew up some ammunition there as he moved toward Charlottesville in 1865. The depot gave rise to two modest resort hotels in the 1920s. The Episcopal church operated Summer's Rest for working people from the Richmond area. The five-story Greenwood Hotel stood beside the depot. Both buildings are gone.

The school was a gift to the community from Randolph Ortman, an estate-owner here in the 1920s. Wealthy residents also gave Greenwood a telephone company and during the Depression provided a soup kitchen for students that served vegetable soup one day and hot chocolate the next.

The country store past the school was owned by D.D.L. Perkins and James Gordon Smith. The general merchandise store was *the* place to shop; it offered everything from groceries, clothing and furniture to candy, paper dolls and paint.

[Note: Newtown Road above Greenwood climbs the Blue Ridge. It offers some stunning views and a visit to Newtown, a hamlet established by blacks, where Ortman built another school that is now a community center. The road ends at Brooksville, the end of this tour.]

Turn left at the post office on Greenwood Road (SR 691) and go one mile to **Mirador,** the estate that was once the childhood home of Nancy Lady Astor. After crossing over I-64, look left to see the barns and the brick mansion.

Built in 1832 by James M. Bowen and acquired in 1894 by Chiswell Langhorne, the house was remodelled in the 1920s according to the plans of William Adams Delano, a New York architect. It is a Virginia Historic Landmark.

Nancy Langhorne, (1879-1964), one of Chiswell's daughters, became the first woman member of the British Parliament when she won the seat for Plymouth vacated by her husband, Waldorf Lord Astor. The Astors risked their lives with their constituents during the World War II bombings, showing grit and grace under pressure.

Turn right onto the Rockfish Gap Turnpike at the stop sign.

The small brick building at this corner was the telephone exchange. The service was supported by local wealthy families and operated by a Mr. Hackett, who reportedly interjected "useful information" into conversations on the party line.

Beyond the **Antiques Center,** just ahead on the left, is the beautiful colonial revival style **Emmanuel Episcopal Church,** now a Virginia Historic Landmark.

The congregation formed in the 18th century. In the mid-1800s a growing number of Episcopalians settled among the already-established Presbyterians in the western county. Six neighbors began the building in 1860; the Bowens of Mirador gave the land. A stroll through the graveyard reveals the names of many early families.

The Langhorne children provided funds to enlarge and remodel Emmanuel in 1911 in honor of their mother. Washington architect Waddy Wood designed the exquisite woodwork. Emmanuel's congregation continues to sponsor outreach programs in the mountain hollows today.

On the right is **Ramsay,** the Gibson estate, most easily seen in winter.

The Langhorne sisters all had looks and personality. One of them, Irene, married artist Charles Dana Gibson and became the first mass media model: the Gibson girl emulated by young women in the 1890s.

On the left in four tenths of a mile look for **Tiverton,** one of the estates that give Greenwood great distinction.

A classical temple in an Edgar Allan Poe setting, Tiverton stands romantically veiled behind trees that encircled a pond between the house and road. Tiverton was built in the early

1900s by Dr. Frederick Owsley, on the site of a house built in the mid-1800s by James M. Bowen for his daughter.

Just past Tiverton, bear right on Brooksville Road (SR 796), part of the old turnpike route, to approach **Lebanon Church** (1747).

Lebanon began as a mission of Mountain Plains Church at Mechums River. Its original communicants were the Scotch-Irish Presbyterians, but the names on the tombstones attest to the fact that soon the membership included many of English ancestry and a few of German background.

In about a mile, Brooksville Road again meets the highway. At the junction is **Brooksville,** a house built by Robert Brooks that was once a busy tavern in a small village.

Brooksville was the all-important junction of the Rockfish Gap and Staunton-James River turnpikes. The Brooksville post office occupied the small building to the right of the house by 1799.

Claudius Crozet boarded at the Brooksville Tavern while he supervised the dangerous construction of the Brooksville railroad tunnel in the 1850s. The workers cut into a soft, rotten slate mixed with red clay rather than the anticipated solid granite; the roof collapsed half way through its 830-foot length and scared the men away from the project. The second half of the tunnel took five years to complete. Crews of Irishmen from New York and New England and later slaves, contracted from their owners, did the work.

General Sheridan camped here on his approach to Charlottesville during his campaign to destroy Confederate food production and supplies. He burned the nearby buildings, saving only the tavern and post office. The town never recovered.

Turn right to follow the turnpike up to Rockfish Gap.

West of Brooksville was an earlier town, now vanished, called New York or Little York. It was founded well before it first appeared on an 1824 map by James Hayes. The first residents were Germans from Pennsylvania. The town had a smithy, tanyard, meeting house, race track and post office. It apparently faded or evolved into Brooksville.

Just beyond the country store in the large barn (on the right), turn left onto Old Turnpike Road (SR 750). The town of **Afton,** lying snug in Rockfish Gap, is about two miles from here, in Nelson County.

The drive passes several old farms with some unique barns, outbuildings and a log cabin. A 1930s service station that serviced the over-heated automobiles climbing to the Blue Ridge Parkway has been recycled as a home.

Near the top of the mountain, at a T-junction, **Afton House** stands amid the antique shops. Once this hotel was the social hub of this area and a summer watering place for heat-stricken Richmonders who stopped at this mountain depot.

Turn right and continue upward as the road crosses the railroad on a wooden bridge and climbs past the shops and depot-turned-professional-building. Turn left after the bridge to visit the depot.

Down the track, out of sight of the depot, is the old Blue Ridge Tunnel of the Louisa Railroad Company. This tunnel, the longest trans-mountain rail tunnel ever built to that time (4,224 feet or 4/5 of a mile), was Claudius Crozet's greatest engineering achievement. Crews at opposite ends worked with pickaxes, black powder and hand drills to chip through quartz, greenstone and granite. They were only a half-inch off center when they broke through at Christmas 1856.

The tunnel, too small for modern trains, was abandoned in 1944. The old tunnel entrance is eighteen feet above the new tunnel.

Turn left on US 250 above Afton and drive 1.2 miles to the top of **Rockfish Gap,** cut by the Rockfish River. Here are the entrances to the **Skyline Drive** (northbound) and the **Blue Ridge Parkway** (stretching southward).

The Rockfish Gap Visitor Center has a tabletop scale model of the parkway and the Valley of Virginia from Harper's Ferry to North Carolina. There is a restaurant here and service station next door.

The tour ends here. Take I-64 back to Charlottesville.

[Note: There are two scenic overlooks on the interstate that are worth a stop if the day is clear. Look for the spire of the Emmanuel Episcopal Church to get an idea of the route you just traveled. In spring and fall, migrating hawks fly past almost at eye level.]

Tour 9   Staunton-James River Turnpike

From Rockfish Gap to Scottsville: 22 miles

From 1826 the Staunton-James River Turnpike linked Staunton
with the James River port at Scottsville and provided Valley farmers and merchants access to Richmond markets. It was an upgrad-
ing of existing roads, and although only a small section of the
roadway was planked, today it bears the name Plank Road for
nearly all of the original route. It joins dramatic mountain land-
scapes with occasional remnants of the small villages that served
the draymen and farmers who traveled this road.

From the Visitors Center, take I-64 westbound 22 miles to Exit 99
(at the apex of the Rockfish Gap in the Blue Ridge Mountain), and
take US 250 east two miles.

> The drive down the steep face of Afton Mountain gives an
> inkling of why state engineer Claudius Crozet, after inspect-
> ing the turnpike in 1840, pronounced the unpaved, steeply-
> graded road a weak commercial link, subject to mud slides
> and washouts. Despite the truth of Crozet's judgment, this
> turnpike funded by private investment, was a great success.
> Produce worth $500,000 annually passed along the precari-
> ous toll route in the 1840s. In the 1850s, however, rail service
> fatally eroded the turnpike's business.

Turn right on Plank Road (SR 692) at **Anderson's Produce.**

> Many fruit stands dotted the highway west of Charlottesville
> when it became a major tourist route to the Skyline Drive in
> the 1930s. Local fruits are still sold here seasonally.

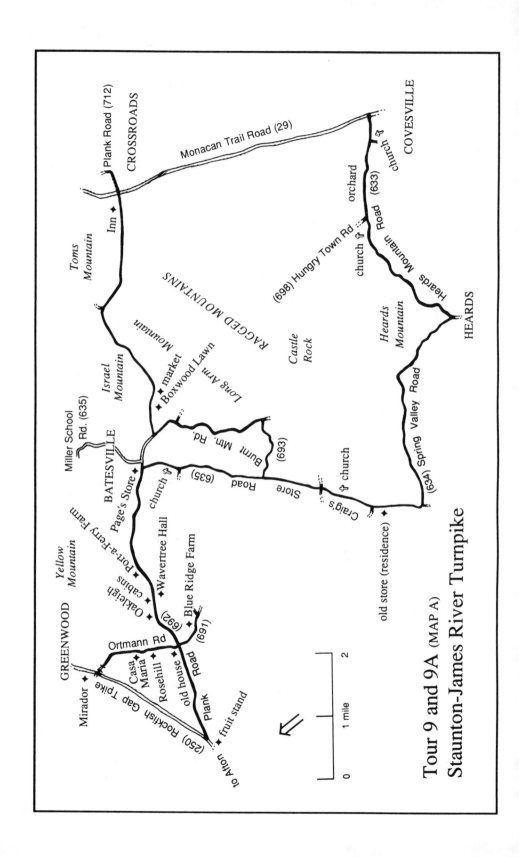

Tour 9 and 9A (MAP A)
Staunton-James River Turnpike

For almost two miles, the turnpike undulates between hedgerows that give it the look of English countryside afloat in a veritable sea of green, with wave after wave rolling to the distant mountains.

> The road roughly follows **Stockton Creek,** one of the sources of Mechums River. The stream bed offered the earliest natural avenue for horse and cart when Scotch-Irish David Stockton crossed the Blue Ridge into this unsettled area in 1734 and built a mill on the creek near here.

At the junction with Ortmann Road (SR 691), turn left to see some of the elegant estates that line the road between here and Mirador.

> The first house on the left, while not one of the grandest on this road, is possibly the oldest house in the county. It dates to the third quarter of the 18th century.

> At the turn of the century a few wealthy families discovered the Greenwood area, which extends several miles north and east from here, as a beautiful spot to build or buy country estates. During the 1920s there were four or five families whose perfected estates were near each other; during the Depression they took an interest in their less fortunate neighbors — truly exhibiting noblesse oblige.

> **Rosehill** was built 1903-30 as a summer home for Gordon Smith and his wife Ella, who founded the April Garden Week Tours, when garden clubs all over the state open their best private gardens and homes to the public. Robert Green, a black artisan, built the dry stone walls that line the road to the Rosehill and Casa Maria estates.

> **Casa Maria** began in the 1920s and was finished by Mrs. W.R. Massie and her daughter (and neighbor) Ella Smith. It was a place of warmth and hospitality, especially for the local school children, who were often invited to parties.

When you reach the bridge over Stockton Creek and the stop sign at Rockfish Gap Turnpike (US 250), turn around and go back to Plank Road.

In the 1930s black congregations celebrated baptisms in the creek below the bridge. Whites joined blacks for the rites and powerful music.

Cross Plank Road and go south on Ortmann Road a quarter of a mile to see **Blue Ridge Farm,** a Virginia Historic Landmark.

The brick mansion with a widow's walk atop its roof sits very near the road, on the left. From 1850-94 it was known at Alton Park and Gluston Park and was owned by the Purcell family. Frederick Owsley bought it in 1894 and sold it to his wife's brother, Randolph Ortman, in 1902. Ortman and his wife hired architect William Lawrence Bottomley, a leader in the restoration of estates, to alter and enlarge this old home.

Evidence of the earliest occupants here—a Native American burial mound—is located nearby, but cannot be seen from the road.

Drive past the house a quarter mile to turn around at the junction with Dick Woods Road (SR 637), another very old country road that follows a buffalo trail. Return to Plank Road and turn right. In a mile, look for **Oakleigh,** on the left.

This huge brick Victorian edifice, built by heirs of the Maxwell House Coffee fortune, is now the home of the Oakleigh Christian Fellowship.

Around a curve, pull off the road at the entrance to the equestrian center, where the road dips to the kind of bottom that Crozet bemoaned as miry in wet weather.

The two cabins across the road exhibit architectural characteristics typical of early Albemarle dwellings. Note the pitch of the roof, the tiny windows, the placement of the chimneys and the thickness of the walls. One room down, may one room up, was about all there was. The cabin with two doors may have been slave quarters.

Dollins Creek crosses the road here and flows through the grounds of mysterious **Wavertree Hall** (1852), well shrouded by foliage behind its securely locked gates.

Quincy A. Shaw II, the brother of Nancy Langhorne's first husband, bought this estate in 1913. The flamboyant Shaw threw himself into local sports and reportedly had cock fights in his formal reception hall.

An old retainer who guarded the estate in the 1970s reported frequent encounters with ghosts. One was a lady he chanced upon when walking in the gardens.

The extensive gardens were restored and flourished in the 1930s and 40s, cared for by later owners, the Churchill Newcombs of Kentucky. The Newcombs were among the founders of the Blue Ridge Hunt Club.

In a quarter of a mile, on the left, is **Port-a-Ferry Farm,** once owned by Judith Gyurky, a Hungarian aristocrat whose life was remarkably daring, courageous and glamorous.

Countess Gyurky, trapped in occupied Hungary during World War II, was determined to escape to the United States with a considerable stable of fine horses of Magyar lineage, bred on the Asian steppes for performance and endurance. Gyurky, a gifted trainer, found an American who sympathized with her goals, married him and thus won entry to the United States as his spouse. What of the horses? The countess spirited them out of Hungary, too, though it took all of her money to do it.

Soon after the war her farmhouse burned. This plucky lady moved into the stable and set up housekeeping among her Magyars.

In a half mile there is a graceful, Queen Anne style 19th-century brick farmhouse, on the right.

In another eight tenths of a miles Plank Road crosses **Stockton's Mill Creek.** The creek, a battered-but-beautiful barn and a corn crib at road's edge announce the entrance to **Batesville,** an important village and toll station on the turnpike.

The early 19th-century **Moon House** or **Layman House,** named for two early owners, is just past the barns, on the left.

This house was once a tavern and stagecoach stop. The locally made brick used in its construction is an especially mellow pink, and the double-porched portico has a lacy sturdiness that creates elegant proportions out of what, if you look closely, is an asymmetrical facade.

The old road passed closer to the front of the building than the modern road; look for the contour evidence on the ground.

Next on the left is the **Batesville United Methodist Church.**

Its first incarnation was as the Midway Chapel, presumably because it was midway between the Brooksville and Crossroads communities in the 1830s. Slave labor built the church (1860), with master carpentry done by local craftsmen James H. Shepherd and John Via. The architecture is a mix of Shenandoah German (two entrances) and Piedmont classic revival (pilasters framing the windows.)

Pull in at **Page's Store** at the junction with Craig's Store Road (SR 635) to savor the essence of this little hamlet.

This 1913 store, the legacy of three generations of Pages, is the sole remnant of commercial activity here, but it is a fine heart for the little community. It maintains the best of its old style and offers contemporary local crafts and a well-stocked deli. Old photos on display reveal Batesville as it once was.

The village, originally known as Mount Israel for nearby Israel Mountain, grew at the fork of Stockton's Mill Creek and Stillhouse Creek on land patented in 1737 by Henry Terrell of Caroline County. By the 1850s, as a result of the business boon engendered by turnpike traffic, there was sufficient population to qualify as an election precinct.

It its heyday Batesville had a post office, toll station, stagecoach stop, inn, stables and stores; even as late as the 1930s there were five stores near this junction.

Two fine houses, the oldest in Batesville, stand diagonally across the road from the store. These early Page family homes date to the 1820s or 1830s. On the 1875 Green-Peyton map, the Page Mill is shown at this location.

Batesville Day, the second Saturday in May, celebrates a renaissance of Batesville that began in the 1960s.

From Page's Store, leave the old turnpike temporarily and drive south on Craig's Store Road. Just across the creek are two elegant, out-of-mainstream mansions.

The first, on the right, evokes an image of an aristocratic, antebellum *grande dame* dressed in white lace with neoclassical fluted underpinnings. On the left is **Castlebrook,** a 19th-century Page home that exhibits its Gothic influence.

A little farther, on a knoll to the right, is the **Mount Ed Baptist Church,** founded in 1788.

> Mount Ed is an offshoot of the Lewis Meeting House and is named for the mountain behind it. The building is an 1840 reconstruction of the original on the site; its design probably influenced that of the Batesville United Methodist Church. Services lapsed in 1943 as Batesville declined and membership diminished, but the congregation is again meeting as the population increases.

Less than a mile past the church are two interesting farmhouses.

> The first house, high on a hill to the right, has an eccentric central tower. The next one, on the left, has an unusual scalloped cornice trim.

The road here seeks ever lower elevations, and at the bottom, at the junction with Burnt Mountain Road (SR 693), is a cabin that backs up on Stockton's Mill Creek.

Optional side trip: If you've ever wanted to visit rustic mountain hollows that seem untouched by time and only lightly brushed by man, this is your chance. Side Trip 9A, an adventure over eight miles of wildly beautiful but unpaved mountain roads, begins here. It bypasses about four miles of turnpike east of Batesville to rejoin this tour at Crossroads. Turn to page 112 for instructions.

To continue this tour, turn left on Burnt Mountain Road. Half a mile along this well-graded gravel road there is a stunning view of the valley and the mountains beyond.

Looking from right to left, you can see **Castle Rock, Long Arm** and **Israel mountains.** These are the main promontories of the **Ragged Mountains,** aptly named for their ragged appearance and all that was dispossessed in this inaccessible corner of the county.

It is thought that Israel Mountain was named for Michael Israel, one of the very few Jewish landowners in early Albemarle. He settled here with his brother and was active in the county militia in the 1750s.

In the midst of orchards, near the stop sign, is an old clapboard house with a long veranda and a shorter, centered, second-story porch. It has a long view to the Blue Ridge and a short view of Long Arm Mountain. Turn left at the stop sign.

Follow Burnt Mountain Road as it descends through orchards and forests and eventually crosses a one-lane bridge over Stillhouse Creek. The road then climbs again, breaks free from the trees, and offers a wonderful view of a fortress-like 19th-century farmhouse.

This was once the main house of a thousand acre farm owned by Clark Wade. The wide, horizontal railings of the double porch echo the lines of its ridge top setting. The brick arches that support the porch cut that line and anchor it firmly to the earth. Notice the dark, glazed brick headers that run in horizontal courses on the end wall.

The site appears quite isolated, but it is only half a mile from Plank Road, near Batesville. When you reach the stop sign, turn right.

[Note: Samuel Miller, the hard working, self educated illegitimate son of a poor widow who lived in a small cabin in a hollow of Israel Mountain, founded the nearby Miller School for indigent boys when he became a wealthy merchant. The school's Victorian buildings, one of which is a Virginia Historical Landmark, were the setting for "Toy Soldiers," a 1991 film starring Lou Gossett, Jr. To visit the school, turn left (back toward Batesville) and then right on Miller School Road (SR 635) about two miles. Backtrack to this point to continue the tour.]

Boxwood Lawn (1860) is one of the few houses along this stretch of Plank Road, but it is a gem. The **Little Market** is a good place to stop for local gossip and a soft drink.

East of the market, the road passes through **Israel's Gap** between Israel and Long Arm mountains. It then angles directly south beside Toms Mountain, named for another early family, in a narrow valley created by the north fork of the Hardware River.

A little over three miles beyond the market, pull off the road to the left, at the gate with the tree farm sign, to see the **Inn at the Crossroads,** a bed and breakfast inn that announced the nearly vanished community of **Crossroads.**

This sturdy brick building (circa 1820) was a tavern built by the Hugh Morris family about the time the road became a turnpike. It was rescued from slow ruin in 1984.

Among the very old outbuildings is a summer kitchen about 30 feet from the house. The original stable was actually inside the lowest level of the tavern, next to the kitchen and dining room, making convenient if close quarters for man and beast. Bedrooms, public rooms and a store filled the three upper floors.

Owner C.G. Sutherland's account book for 1852 lists the community's purchases from hay to whiskey. Sutherland kept the post office in his store. This was a voter precinct by mid-19th century.

There was an Anglican church here as early as the 1770s. the church you see today (just past the inn) was completed in 1835. It served as a nondenominational church until 1892, when it was converted to a schoolhouse. It continued in that capacity for another thirty years.

Crossroads was in decline by the end of the 1920s, but even during the Depression thirty-five black men of the neighborhood successfully supported St. Lukes, a fraternal benevolent society that also functioned as an insurance company for its members.

Continue to the stop sign at Monacan Trail Road (US 29), a four-lane, divided highway.

This was the Old Lynchburg Road, also called Wheeler's Road, a north-south connector that linked the south end of the county with Charlottesville in 1820.

Cross the highway and continue on Plank Road. In a third of a mile you will pass a group of old log cabins. Just beyond the cabins, near the road, is a stucco building, part of an old mill complex. The road bridges a creek here, a feeder of the Hardware River.

Continue to follow Plank Road, but notice that the road number changes to SR 712 beyond the Methodist church. This is still the old Staunton-James River Turnpike route.

Over the next mile and seven tenths, enjoy views of **Carter's Mountain,** on the left, and **Green Mountain.**

North Garden, under the dome of **Gay Mountain,** was the junction of the turnpike and the Southern Railroad line (1863), making it an agricultural shipping point.

President Theodore Roosevelt arrived here by train from Washington, D.C., to visit his cabin retreat near Keene.

Applejack brandy was a home brew specialty made in Virginia from its earliest days. Laird's Applejack, widely distributed, is still produced in North Garden.

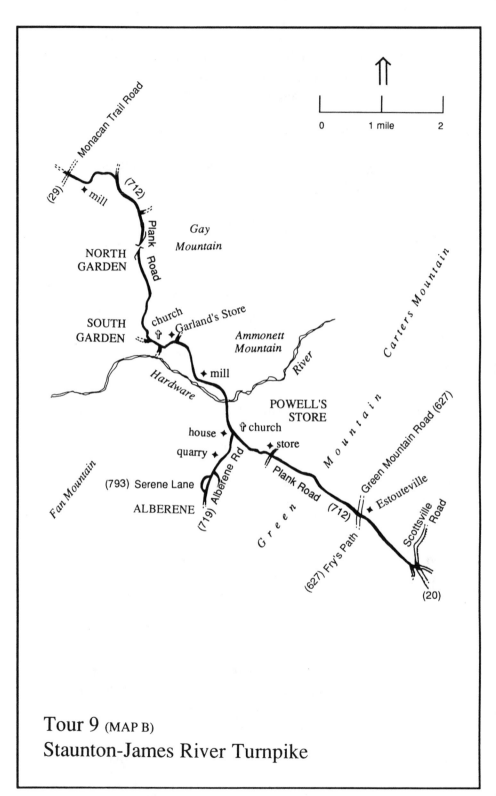

Tour 9 (MAP B)
Staunton-James River Turnpike

Beware the curves in the road for the two miles between North Garden and its opposite number, **South Garden.**

The south fork of the Hardware River runs beside the road near the turn-of-the-century **South Garden Baptist Church** at the entrance to South Garden.

Ammonett Mountain is to the left, and **Fan Mountain,** the location of the University of Virginia's large telescope, is to the right.

Continue less than half a mile beyond South Garden to **Garland's Store** at the junction with the Old Lynchburg Road (SR 631).

This clapboard building was originally a toll house on the turnpike. A wagon hauling wheat paid a typical toll of 46 cents in 1831. At a later period the building housed an orphanage. As Garland's Store, it gave its name to the neighborhood.

In another mile, there is a place to pull off the road beside the **Hardware River.** Stop here for a few minutes to savor your surroundings.

This is the beginning of a spectacular stretch of read that follows the largest and strongest waterway within the southern half of Albemarle.

From the mid to the late 17th century many immigrants arrived in Virginia from Yorkshire, England. The name Hardware probably evolved from the name of the famous scenic spot in Yorkshire, a water passage called the Hardwarl.

The sturdy building ahead on the left is the miller's house for **Cocke's Mill.**

The mill, known successively as Cocke's, Coles's and Johnson's, was built in 1792 by Major James Powell Cocke, who moved here from Henrico County. The original patentee of this land was Mildred Meriwether, the daughter of Nicholas Meriwether, who owned much land in northeastern Albemarle.

A half mile past the mill is the junction with Alberene Road (SR 719). Turn right for a brief diversion from the turnpike.

In about four tenths of a mile, right beside the road, is part of the quarry that gave rise to the town of **Alberene** in the 1880s.

> Albemarle boasts the largest deposit of soapstone on the east coast. The Native Americans preceded the Europeans in appreciating the heat retaining qualities of this smooth, dense, gray/green stone. A stove made from it releases its heat slowly and evenly.
>
> In the industrial boom of the late 19th century, modern quarrying techniques came to this deposit. The Alberene Stone Company exhausted the potential here and moved to its other branch in Schuyler, just over the line in Nelson County.
>
> Some of the industrial buildings and company houses remain, reminders of the former bustle and prosperity here.

For a short circle tour through this tiny community, drive on past the quarry and turn right on Serene Lane (SR 793), then left when it reconnects with Alberene Road. Stumptown Road (SR 792) is a dead end that leads to a cluster of company houses.

Return to Plank Road. Before you turn right, note the **Alberene Baptist Church** (1901) and another of the company houses at the junction.

The church served the quarry workers and their families. The Alberene Lodge, an ubiquitous feature of small community life at the turn of the century, stands beside the church.

At the junction with Secretary's Sand Road (SR 717), in about eight tenths of a mile, are two very old buildings; the one on the right has a double level porch.

This is the crossroads of **Powell's Store,** which, like Garland's Store, was named for an early emporium. The village grew up on the first large grant of land in the southern part of the county, that patented by the Eppes family.

About 1.5 miles from Powell's Store is the junction with SR 627, to the left called Fry's Path and to the right called Green Mountain Road. On the left is **Estouteville,** a Coles's family plantation better seen on tour 11.

Frances Eppes patented 6,500 acres on the Hardware River in 1730, one of the earliest patents and one of the largest in what was to become Albemarle. A few years later, the Eppes family sold 3,000 acres to John Coles of Henrico.

Plank Road meets Scottsville Road (VA 20), in another mile and a half. Two old country stores signal your arrival in **Keene.**

The turnpike continued to the wharves in Scottsville, but this tour ends here. Scottsville is explored in Tour 13.

To return to Charlottesville, about sixteen miles north, turn left on Scottsville Road.

Side Trip 9A   Mountain Hollows

Batesville to Heards: 16 miles

Listen for the faint ringing of mountain banjos as, like Alice, you pass through an imaginary rabbit hole into the wonderland of the Ragged Mountains. Missions, old stores and cabins dot the trail over oak ridges and through quintessential mountain hollows. A four-wheel-drive vehicle is not necessary, but be warned that in inclement weather this narrow, unpaved, winding and sometimes steep mountain road can be a challenge.

[The map for this side trip is on page 98.] Continue on Craig's Store Road (SR 635) a mile and three tenths past Burnt Mountain Road (SR 693), and pull in at the American Gothic **Holy Cross Church**, which began as a missionary outpost early in this century.

> Deaconess Margaretta James and Miss Hallie Worsham, whose house stands beside the chapel, came from Richmond in 1918 to serve this isolated mountain area. They founded the mission and built the Episcopal chapel, an outpost of Emmanuel Church in Greenwood.

> Miss Hallie painted the lilies on the baptismal font, which can be seen through the side door. The sanctuary is on a very small scale; there are ceiling fans and individual hand fans in the dark wooden pews. Members of Emmanuel church fund a food bank from the new kitchen adjoining the chapel.

> In the old parish hall, recently razed, local residents attended bazaars, Christmas pageants, roller skating and bowling par-

ties, dances and Friday night movies. The **Deaconess House**, the stucco house near the chapel, was both home to the missionaries and the meeting place for services before the chapel was built.

In six tenths of a mile, on the right and almost in the road, is the old **Bunch Store**, later called **Craig's Store** and now a private residence.

> This store was owned and operated by the Bunch family, many of whom are buried in the Holy Cross cemetery. Teora Bunch married Julius Craig in the 19th century and the store then took Craig's name. Its architectural lines suggest an origin in the 18th century.

The road from here draws you farther into the wilderness. When you reach Spring Valley Road (SR 634) in eight tenths of a mile, you will have already passed into Nelson County.

The real adventure begins with a left turn onto Spring Valley Road. For the first two miles the road passes through woods and orchards and offers an occasional view of the mountains.

> The road follows **Perry Creek** on the southern side of **Castle Rock,** the mountain on your left.

> The orchard is in **Spring Valley.** In the fall the gnarled limbs are laden with luscious red apples, as wickedly tempting as those in a fairy tale by the Brothers Grimm.

> It is in this mood that you come upon a lake that seems poised to flood the road. In this fantastic landscape it seems you are alone with the apple trees, but reality intrudes in the guise of a few worn farm buildings, migrant worker quarters and a railway spur line for transporting the fruit.

Now the road begins to climb into an old oak forest that once rang with the woodsman's axe.

> Timbering was one of the only livelihoods in the steeper terrains of Albemarle. The road edges the southern slopes of **Heards Mountain**. An occasional cabin punctuates the next mile.

As the road begins to descend, the cabins grow more frequent and the mailboxes repeat family names whose histories are as old as Albemarle. The tiny village of **Heards** suddenly materializes in a wide, open bowl surrounded by mountains. Heards is at the junction of Spring Valley Road and Heards Mountain Road (SR 633).

> The only store in Heards, now a home, stands severely vertical, as if influenced by the surrounding mountains, at the junction. Scattered around it are a handful of small homes.

> Stelling banjos are made at the farm on the branch of Heards Mountain Road that bears right at the store. This instrument, appropriate to its rustic birthplace, is famous in bluegrass music circles.

Turn left at the store on Heards Mountain Road, which existed by 1745. The roads climbs sharply along a shelf not made for passing. Where it finally broadens, there is a good view of the Stelling farm and the village of Heards below.

The road threads through a narrow mountain gap, levels out and then begins its descent past homes tucked away in private pockets. When pavement appears, rest assured you have returned to civilization.

The **Bethel Methodist Church** stands at the junction with Hungry Town Road (SR 698) — its historic name.

The stream seen at the junction is the source of the south fork of the Hardware River. Note the old one-room log structure opposite the church. It has a brick and stone chimney.

Follow the fence a quarter of a mile along Heards Road as it passes the **Highland Orchards,** where you can pick your own fruit in season.

The views here open out to distant mountains and encourage the reassuring thought that life is not always so razor edge as in the mountain coves.

Just three miles from Heards, though light years away in time, is a cluster of modern ranchers and the brick **Covesville Baptist Church** (1893) on the right.

This is the third of three churches near Ragged Mountain passes, all dating to the turn of the century. Missionaries of the period saw the need to bring education, medicine and spiritual comfort to the mountain dwellers left behind in the industrialization of the country.

Three-tenths of a mile from the church is the junction with Monacan Trail Road (US 29). Turn left and drive 4.3 miles to the junction with Plank Road (SR 692) at Crossroads. Turn right to re-join Tour 9 on page 107.

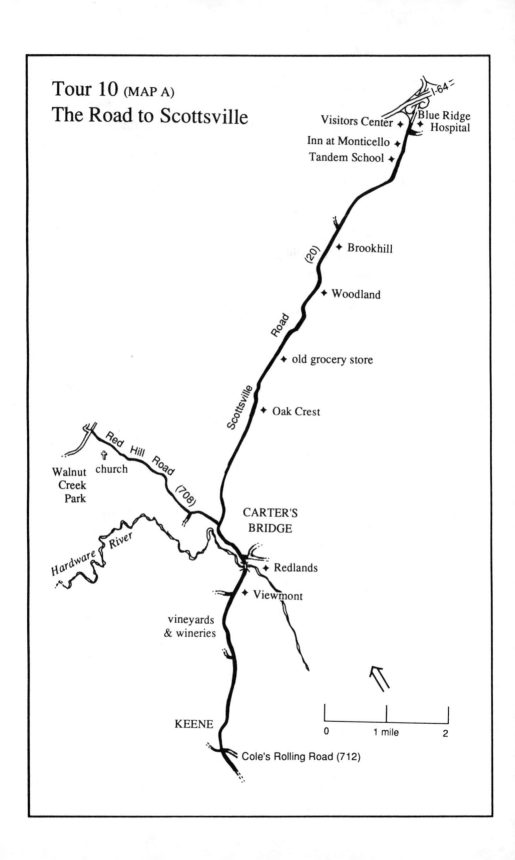

Tour 10 (MAP A)
The Road to Scottsville

I-64

Visitors Center ✦ ✦ Blue Ridge
Hospital
Inn at Monticello ✦
Tandem School ✦

(20) ✦ Brookhill

✦ Woodland

✦ old grocery store

Scottsville Road ✦ Oak Crest

Red Hill Road ⸸ church
Walnut
Creek
Park (708)

Hardware River

CARTER'S
BRIDGE

✦ Redlands

✦ Viewmont

vineyards
& wineries

KEENE

0   1 mile   2

Cole's Rolling Road (712)

Tour 10   Scottsville Road

Charlottesville to Scottsville: 22 miles

The Scottsville Road connected the northern Albemarle plantations to the courthouse when Scottsville was the county seat
(1741-61). Today it is a Virginia scenic byway called the Consti-
tution Highway, a status that honors and preserves its beauty.

This tour begins at the traffic signal at the junction of the
Scottsville Road (VA 20) and the entrance to the Visitors Center.

> Opposite the Visitors Center are the grounds of the **Blue
> Ridge Hospital,** the University of Virginia rehabilitation
> center, and the landing area for Pegasus, the university's res-
> cue helicopter. They lie at the base of Carter's Mountain,
> known in Jefferson's day as Mount Alto and more recently as
> **Brown's Mountain.**
>
> In the 1730s, John Carter was the Secretary of the colony of
> Virginia, the official who controlled the granting of land
> patents. Of all the land available to him in this area, he chose
> Mount Alto for its strategic location at the passage through
> the Southwest Mountains and for the mineral deposits he
> hoped lay buried there. Carter's grant totaled more than 9,000
> acres.
>
> During a 1920s nationwide tuberculosis epidemic, 300 pa-
> tients spent an average of two and a half years in treatment
> here. Kenneth Heatwole, M.D., the staff doctor 1951-86,
> came here when as a medical student he himself contracted
> the disease. He achieved a cure and then worked to eliminate
> the stigma and ostracism tuberculosis patients suffered.

Turn right and proceed south on the Scottsville Road. On the right, just past Willow Lake Drive, is **The Inn at Monticello**, an antique-filled bed and breakfast inn.

Three tenths of a mile past the inn is the **Tandem School**, its entrance sign graced with an evergreen tree.

> Tandem's past includes a link to medicine. In 1903 Paul B. Barringer, M.D., turned this 1838 house, then called Verdant Lawn, into a sanitarium. Barringer taught at the University of Virginia Medical School and headed a drive to establish a teaching hospital around 1900. The private clinics building at the university is named in his honor.
>
> Since 1974, Verdant Lawn has been home to a small private school (grades 5-12) that operates under the premise that students will thrive in an atmosphere of freedom and responsibility.

Beyond Tandem are two very old houses, both built in the early 19th century by Jefferson's carpenters and both on the left side of the road. The first house is about a mile and a half from Tandem, three tenths of a mile past the junction with Avon Street (SR 742).

> Look for the entrance to **Brookhill,** a horse farm. The pre-1841 farmhouse can be most easily seen in winter. James Minor built the house. Dr. Charles Minor conducted a school for boys here after 1857. The university had a polo field here for many years.
>
> **Woodland** (1810) is almost a mile past Brookhill. The road swings right and then left again to curve around its property.

Just over a mile from Woodland is the clapboard **Thomas's Grocery,** on the left.

No longer in use, the store was once vital to the area. Notice the diagonal boards in the doors, a nice detail of construction.

In another mile, look for the derelict remnants of an abandoned tavern on a wooded knoll to the left. **Oak Crest** dates from before the Revolution and was owned by Pleasant Sowell.

A mile and a half farther, turn right on Red Hill Road (SR 708). Go 2.5 miles to see the **Hardware Baptist Church** (1802).

Lottie Moon of nearby Viewmont plantation, is well known among the Southern Baptists as a missionary to China in the mid-19th century. She is remembered by the offering taken for overseas missions at Christmas in Baptist churches. Her family attended this church.

The small cemetery behind the church has some slate headstones that were apparently not done by a professional monument carver. One of them, located near the back fence, reads:

APRIL 1916
MR JACK
RIPLEY
DIAD THE
10
OF APRIL
BIRAID AT
HIRDWER
THUCH

About a mile past the church is **Walnut Creek Park.** There are adequate signs to guide you to it.

> A county park opened in 1992, it offers picnic areas and facilities for swimming, canoeing and fishing. There is an entrance fee.

Return to the Scottsville Road and turn right. In nearly a mile you will cross **Carter's Bridge**, which gives its name to this farm neighborhood where several old roads converged in this narrow break in the Southwest Mountains.

> Secretary Carter's mountain property ended at the Hardware River. The ford was named for Robert Davis, Carter's overseer, who capitalized on its strategic location. Since Carter was an absentee owner, it was Davis who strongly influenced the routing of the roads in this part of the county and supervised Carter's slaves, who did most of the work. They built a mill here in the 1730s or 40s, the Secretary's Mill.
>
> In 1746 the Albemarle court ordered a road be built south from the mill to Scottsville, then called Secretary's Road, now the Scottsville Road.
>
> Slaves were very much in demand in the Piedmont in the mid-18th century for the laborious cultivation of tobacco and for building houses, mills and roads. At that time, more than half of the slaves in Virginia lived west of the fall line. During the last 25 years of the slave trade, the Piedmont took all of the new arrivals.
>
> Around 1800, no more than three or four planters in the county owned more than 100 slaves, while most owned none. A farmer who owned 100 to 200 acres may have had a slave or two, but he and his family provided most of their own labor.

The fence of the vast **Viewmont** plantation begins at Carter's Bridge and stretches to the south about a mile and a half. A Virginia Historic Landmark marker stands at the farm entrance, eight tenths of a mile from the bridge.

Today's house stands on the site of the original, which burned early in this century.

Joshua Fry, born 1699 in Somersetshire, England, acquired this plantation sometime before 1744. Fry came to Virginia as a mathematics professor at William and Mary College, but was disqualified from that position once he married. With a reputation for outstanding knowledge and skill, he was appointed a surveyor, a lucrative post on the frontier and a great vantage point from which to observe the expanding geographic edge of Virginia.

Fry served as Albemarle's burgess in the capital and was chosen to command the Virginia militia in the French and Indian War. George Washington was his second in command. Fry died of a fever during a 1754 campaign in Maryland. On the tree that marked his grave, Washington carved, "Here lies the good, the just, and the noble Fry."

A later owner of Viewmont was Virginia governor Edmund Randolph, who purchased the property in 1786 and lived here for 12 years.

Lottie Moon was born at Viewmont in 1843 and grew up on the estate.

About eight tenths of a mile past the entrance to Viewmont is the junction with Harris Creek Road (SR 720). Vineyards offering wine tasting and tours are about a half mile down this road .

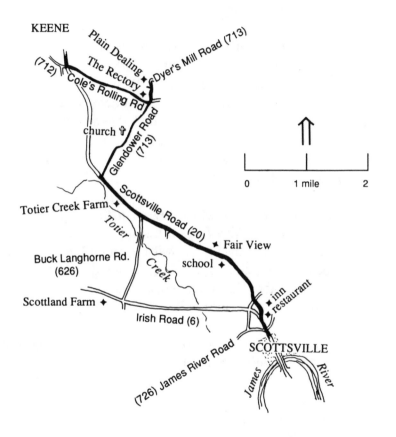

KEENE

Plain Dealing

(712)

The Rectory ✦ Dyer's Mill Road (713)

Cole's Rolling Rd

church ✝

Glendower Road (713)

Totier Creek Farm ✦

Scottsville Road (20)

Buck Langhorne Rd. (626)

Totier

Creek

school ✦

Fair View ✦

Scottland Farm ✦

Irish Road (6)

inn

restaurant

(726) James River Road

SCOTTSVILLE

James

River

Tour 10 (MAP B)
The Road to Scottsville

Continue south on the Scottsville Road a mile and a half to the crossroads community of **Keene** at the junction of the Scottsville Road and the old Staunton-James River Turnpike (SR 712). Eastward from here it is now called Cole's Rolling Road.

> There is a general store and gas station here that offers diesel fuel as well as gasoline.

Turn left on Cole's Rolling Road.

> Rolling roads were built so that barrels of tobacco, called hogsheads, could be rolled to the wharves on the James River, thus eliminating the need for heavy wagons that were easily mired.

For about two miles you will pass fences belonging to Plain Dealing, another vast estate described below. In two and a half miles, Cole's Rolling Road jogs left around the grounds of **The Rectory.**

> This house is the 1839 manse of nearby Christ Church Glendower. The house is best seen from through its front gate, around the turn.

Just past The Rectory bear left on Dyer's Mill Road (SR 713) to the entrance of **Plain Dealing,** around the bend.

> Plain Dealing, a Virginia Historic Landmark, was Samuel Dyer's plantation house and store. Bypassed now by modern highways, this intersection on the old road was a main center of commerce in the 18th and 19th centuries.

> Dyer emigrated from Bristol, England, as an indentured servant at 14 and served in the Revolution. He began his career as a merchant when he built his house and store here in 1787. The name was taken from a sign that once hung above the entrance to the store.

Bishop J.P.B. Wilmer owned the house after 1840. It was while visiting Wilmer after the Civil War that his friend Robert E. Lee made his decision to accept the presidency of Washington College (now Washington and Lee University) in Lexington, Virginia.

Theodore Roosevelt's wife was a friend of one of Plain Dealing's later owners. She bought a few acres of the plantation's forest and built a rustic, two-room cabin, Pine Knot, where the family could hunt, fish and enjoy nature. The family came several times while Teddy was president and lived without electricity or indoor plumbing.

Backtrack past The Rectory and continue straight on unpaved Glendower Road (SR 713) to see one of the loveliest churches in Albemarle, **Christ Church Glendower**.

Christ Church was the main church of St. Anne's parish, a geographic territory of the Anglican church, carved from Goochland County's St. James parish in 1745. The first rector, Robert Rose, left a vivid diary of his visits in his frontier parish. Thomas Jefferson served on the vestry here.

The church was built in 1832 by William B. Phillips, a carpenter and mason Jefferson had employed at the University of Virginia. Phillips also built the Madison County and Green County courthouses.

Continue past the church a little more than a mile to regain the Scottsville Road. Turn left.

The 400-acre glebe for Glendower adjoined this junction on **Totier Creek,** an important tributary of the nearby James River. There was a mill here, called successively Scott's, Dyer's, and Dawson's mill. (The creek may be hidden at this point. You'll see it as you drive on.)

The land here was originally patented by Edward Scott, a member of the family for whom Scottsville was named; his nearby farm was named Glendower. Albemarle's first county government was chosen at a meeting at Glendower, a modest house then owned by Scott's widow. Joshua Fry was appointed militia commander. Peter Jefferson was the county surveyor, William Randolph was the county clerk and Joseph Thompson was the sheriff.

Drive half a mile south on the Scottsville Road and look to the right to see the roof of **Totier** (pronounced Totel) **Creek Farm**, built between 1827 and 1875 by William H. Dyer, the heir of Samuel of Plain Dealing.

Colonel Charles Chiswell operated a forge on Scotland Farm, his plantation not far to the south of here. This was recently confirmed by the discovery of bars of pig iron on the site, one of the rare spots in the county where Secretary Carter's hopes for mineral resources was fulfilled.

A mile and seven tenths past Totier Creek Farm, on the left, is **Fair View**, the farm once owned by John Manahan, one of Charlottesville's most interesting eccentrics. A gazebo sits between the house and the road.

The beautiful three-part white house was designed by restoration architect Milton Grigg for Jack Manahan before World War II.

Manahan, who held a Ph.D. in history, owned several inherited properties including Fair View, which his father had developed into one of the most progressive and successful dairy farms in the region.

Manahan was obsessed with genealogical puzzles; he could remember intricate relationships among Virginians over the first 300 years of settlement as well as royal lineages. His wife, Anna Anderson, claimed to be Anastasia, the sole survivor of the Bolshevik assassination of Czar Nicholas II's family during the Russian Revolution. Her complicated claim must have been like catnip to him.

Manahan was Anastasia's caretaker during her equally eccentric life. They were often seen on this road as he chauffeured his wizened princess in a derelict pickup truck, he in a kilt and tam-o-shanter, she swathed in odd bits of exotic drapery.

Beyond Fairview the road begins its decent into Scottsville, about a mile away. Just past the junction with James River Road (SR 726), look left to see the entrance to **High Meadows Inn**, a bed and breakfast inn hidden on the hill above **Lumpkin's Restaurant.**

High Meadows was built in 1831 by owner and surveyor Peter White. C.B. Harris, a Scottsville businessman, built a second house in 1882 to accommodate his large family. His wife wanted to keep the old house, so a long hallway was built to link the two houses.

Mrs. Lumpkin's restaurant is beside the inn's entrance. Known for its Virginia Piedmont style Southern cooking, it is a good place to have lunch (closed Wednesdays).

This tour ends here, on the ridge above Scottsville. Tour 11 explores the town. To return to Charlottesville, take the Scottsville Road north.

Tour 11   Scottsville and the Canal Towns

Scottsville to Schuyler 14.4 miles

Scottsville, Albemarle's oldest town, is on a great horseshoe bend in the James River at its northernmost point. Even before the Europeans arrived, the Monacans had a settlement here. Scott's Landing, as the town was first called, was centrally located when it served as the county seat from 1745 to 1761.

During the Revolution, colonial arms were stored in the courthouse at Scott's Landing. The marquis de Lafayette and his men saved the munitions and county records from destruction by British forces under Colonel John Graves Simcoe. This was an important turning point in the war, diverting the British east to the final confrontation at Yorktown.

After the Revolution, George Washington and other leaders of the young nation saw the vital need to link commerce from the Mississippi Valley to the Atlantic states. By the end of 1789, the canals built around the fall of the James at Richmond permitted uninterrupted travel and ushered in an era of flourishing river trade to the Piedmont. With the coming of the James River-Kanawha Canal and the Staunton-James River Turnpike, the town grew and prospered and changed its name to Scottsville.

During the Civil War, Scottsville's prosperity attracted General Sheridan, who rampaged through Virginia with 10,000 soldiers, burning Confederate storehouses and disrupting supply lines. He destroyed the canal locks, effectively plugging the Confederate's main supply route.

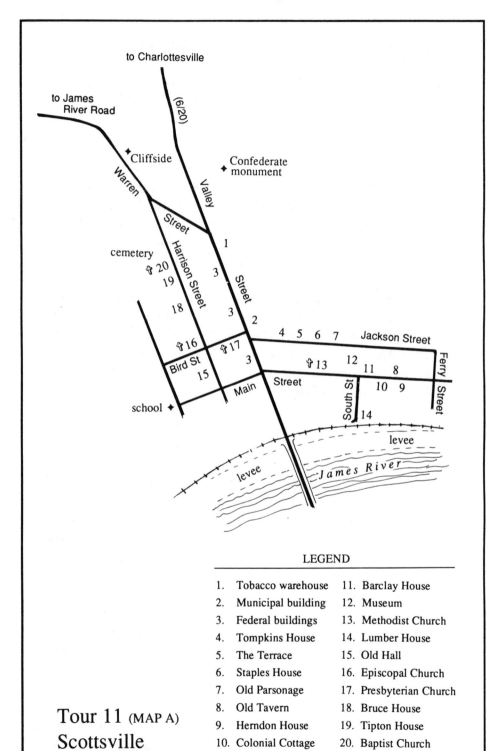

to Charlottesville

to James
River Road

(6/20)

◆Cliffside

Warren

◆ Confederate
monument

Valley

Street

Harrison Street

cemetery

✞ 20
19

18

1

3

Street

3

2

✞ 16

✞ 17

Bird St

15

3

4 5 6 7   Jackson Street

✞ 13

12
11   8

Main   Street

South St

10   9

school ◆

14

levee

levee

James River

Ferry Street

LEGEND

1.	Tobacco warehouse	11.	Barclay House
2.	Municipal building	12.	Museum
3.	Federal buildings	13.	Methodist Church
4.	Tompkins House	14.	Lumber House
5.	The Terrace	15.	Old Hall
6.	Staples House	16.	Episcopal Church
7.	Old Parsonage	17.	Presbyterian Church
8.	Old Tavern	18.	Bruce House
9.	Herndon House	19.	Tipton House
10.	Colonial Cottage	20.	Baptist Church

Tour 11 (MAP A)
Scottsville

The destruction of the canal signaled the demise of Scottsville as a commercial center. In 1880 a railroad company, today's Chesapeake and Ohio, purchased the James River-Kanawha Canal Company and laid a track along the abandoned towpath to the New River gorge; the railroad replaced the river traffic, but Scottsville was not a major depot.

This tour begins in Scottsville, about 18 miles south of the Visitors Center on the Scottsville Road (VA 20). As you enter the town from the north, take note of the many original buildings that line the few blocks of downtown.

> The three-story brick warehouse (1850) about midway down the street on the left is a particularly fine example of early republic building. Scottsville has a large concentration of federal architecture, some 32 buildings.

> The cafe on the right, **The Pig & Steak,** is the former Dew Drop Inn, where TV's John Boy and his siblings stopped on their weekly shopping excursions from Walton's Mountain. **Granny A's** boasts a more recent celebrity sighting: Sam Shepherd took Bob Dylan there for the good eats.

Stay on Valley Street as it crosses the river, but at the first safe opportunity, turn around and recross the bridge. As you enter Scottsville from the south, the bridge offers a comprehensive view of the river, the railroad and the town.

> To the left (upriver about a mile) were the courthouse, a ferry from the courthouse to the south bank of the James and a tavern, all located on property patented by Daniel and Edward Scott in 1732. John Lewis, the community banker and mill owner, operated a tavern near the courthouse.

> Peter Jefferson owned a tavern and a farm, Snowden, on the south side of the river; his son Randolph later lived there.

Scottish factors, who purchased tobacco from local planters, set up shop on the waterfront.

Look to the right to see the modern levee (1989), designed to control the flooding that almost destroyed the town four times in this century.

Go back over the bridge, through the intersection with Main Street, and turn right onto narrow Jackson Street, just past the service station.

Jackson climbs steeply past four early houses, then descends as it curves back to Main. The old River Road originally skirted the river above this high ledge.

The **Tompkins House** (1800) is a story-and-a-half in the federal style. **The Terrace** (1897) is a two-story Victorian. The **Staples House** (1840) has the original beaded weatherboarding. The fourth house served as the **Old Methodist Parsonage** for several years after the church purchased it in 1885 for $1,000.

At the bottom of the hill, turn right onto Main Street. On the right is the **Old Tavern** (late 1700s) with a double front porch. On the left are two 18th-century houses.

The **Herndon House** (1790-1810) has a chimney at either end and a front-to-back central passage, typical of Virginia architecture of the time. The **Colonial Cottage,** possibly the oldest structure in Scottsville, has the original beaded siding with rose-headed nails. The front dates to 1780; the back section is older.

At the junction with South Street are the **Barclay House,** the **Scottsville Museum** and the **Scottsville United Methodist Church,** all on the right.

The Barclay House was built about 1830 by Thomas Staples. James Barclay, an uncle of the missionary Lottie Moon and the founder and first pastor of the church next door, lived here from the late 1830s to 1851. He bought Monticello at auction after Jefferson's death in 1826, but found it difficult to live there because of the curiousity seekers. In 1851 he was chosen to be the first missionary from the United States to Jerusalem. President Franklin Pierce appointed him an inventor for the U.S. mint, where he devised ways to foil counterfeiters and prevent the deterioration of coins.

The Disciples church next door dates to 1846. Now a museum, it houses a wonderfully eccentric collection of town memorabilia, the kind of museum every town with such a colorful history should have.

The Scottsville Methodist church fits well in Barclay's community. Methodism swept Virginia during the years immediately following the Revolution, an emotive offspring of the Anglican church.

The **Lumber House** is one block toward the river from the museum, beside the levee at the foot of South Street.

The three-story warehouse (circa 1830) sat beside the canal. The "lumber" in its name was not necessarily wood; the word meant anything that needed storing. General Sheridan burned this and other warehouses here in March 1865. It was repaired in 1871 by a passenger packet line; that is probably when the gambrel roof was added.

Continue on Main, cross Valley Street and turn right on Harrison Street, which boasts several very fine federal townhomes.

Immediately to the left, behind the white picket fence, is **Old Hall,** built in 1830 by James W. Mason for his bride. It was designed by Benjamin H. Magruder, an architect who worked with Jefferson. There is evidence that Hessians, former prisoners of war at The Barracks, worked on the house.

A later family in residence, the Beals, lived here for 100 years and gave Scottsville her mayors for 30 years. During the Union's occupation of Scottsville, Sheridan's staff officer, General Wesley Merritt, quartered here while his troops wrecked the canals.

Drs. John and Orianna Moon Andrews operated a hospital here from 1879 to 1883. Orianna was Lottie Moon's sister and also served as a missionary in Jerusalem.

At the next intersection, Bird Street, is **St. John's Episcopal Church** (1875), a perfect American Gothic beauty.

Half a block to the right on Bird is the elegant brick **Scottsville Presbyterian Church,** the oldest in the area. The congregation organized in 1827, built the church in 1832.

In another block, very close to the street on the left, the **Bruce House** is easily identified by its elevated temple porch.

Another federal design, it was built about 1820 by the Jefferies family. The story-and-a-half home has a raised English basement that offers additional living space.

Beyond Bruce House is **Tipton House** and the 1840 **Scottsville Baptist Church.**

The church was used as a Confederate hospital during the Civil War. It was remodeled in 1930.

From the front steps of the church, look across the town to the granite obelisk on the hillside. This marks the final resting place of Confederates who died in the hospitals of Scottsville 1861-65. It is dedicated to the memory of Colonel Henry Gantt, Major James C. Hill and the "officers and men of Southern Albemarle who fought under the Stars and Bars of the Confederacy."

Drive down the hill to the stop sign. Bear left on Warren Street (SR 1302). On the right are the brick pillars topped with eagles that mark the entrance to **Cliffside,** a Virginia Historic Landmark and a private home.

John Lewis II, a banker and tavern keeper, built this house in 1785-1810 on land his family patented in 1741. Cliffside served as General Sheridan's headquarters while he was in Scottsville. General Custer, who was on Sheridan's staff, also quartered here.

This ends the tour of Scottsville. Continue on Warren Street to the stop sign at the James River Road (SR 726).

Chester, an 1847 house with some rare old specimen trees on its grounds, is a bed and breakfast inn about a tenth of a mile to the right.

From Warren Street, turn left on the James River Road seven tenths of a mile, where a sign on the left marks the private drive into **Valmont,** once known as Belle Grove, where the county's first courthouse, jail and ferry at Scott's Landing were located.

Daniel Scott owned Belle Grove in 1745, when it was chosen as the site for the courthouse. He profited by establishing varied commercial enterprises here. Scottsville is named for him.

Hatton Grange, noted on the sign, was a neighboring estate belonging to former governor Wilson Cary Nicholas.

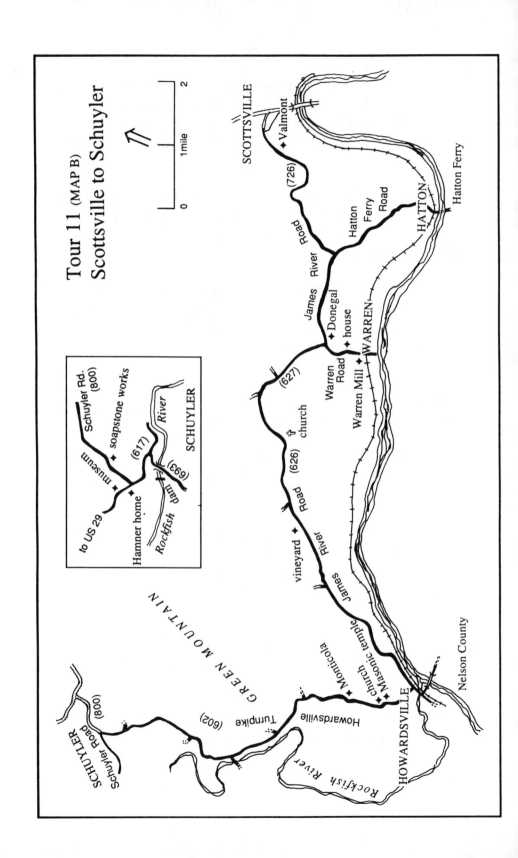

Tour 11 (MAP B)
Scottsville to Schuyler

About two miles beyond Valmont, turn left on Hatton Ferry Road (SR 625) and continue another two miles to **Hatton,** to see a remnant of the James River-Kanawha Canal and one of the rare poled barge ferries still in operation in the United States.

As you enter Hatton, you will come to a crossing of the CSX railroad tracks. Before crossing the track, look for a very narrow, deep ditch running parallel to the track on the left. This is what remains of the **canal;** the track itself is on what was the **towpath.**

This is the headquarters for the **James River Runners,** tubing and canoe trip operators and outfitters. In the office there are topographical maps showing canal sites. If they're not busy with customers, the staff can direct you to a stone **culvert** about 120 feet east of the building that carried a stream beneath the canal. **Lock number 24** is also nearby.

In mid-June there is a bateaux traffic reenactment on the James River with an overnight camp and entertainment at Hatton.

Walk across the track and down the road to the river to see the **Hatton Ferry.** Stop at the operator's building for a little more canal history in an interesting display.

This free ferry has been plying the James for more than 100 years. It carries both pedestrians and vehicles between April 15 and October 15 when the water level is neither too high nor too low. Author Earl Hamner and "John Boy Walton" star Richard Thomas were on hand when the ferry was rededicated in 1976.

Backtrack a couple of miles to the stop sign; go straight ahead to stay on the James River Road. In 1.4 miles, on the left, look for **Donegal,** once the Nicholas family home.

Governor Nicholas established the town of Warren at the river landing on his thriving plantation, but his high hopes for the town's potential were unrealized.

The plantation house is a wonderful amalgam of parts, including a huge room that is a small scale replica of Christ Church Glendower.

Immediately past Donegal, bear left on Warren Road (SR 627) and drive into **Warren,** about a mile.

Look for the **William Walker House** in about a half mile. It is a small, Jefferson-inspired brick residence, on the left. This little jewel was built in the early 18th century by the owner's brother, who built for Jefferson, and is a Virginia Historic Landmark.

As you reach the southern end of the cluster of houses that is Warren today, the road descends to the railroad track. Park near the road.

Canal lock 25 lies buried beneath Warren Road on this side of the tracks.

Walk a few hundred feet to the **Ballinger Creek culvert.** You will know you are standing over one of the best preserved remnants of the James River-Kanawha Canal when you hear and see the creek flowing beneath the road and track. This culvert once carried the creek beneath the canal itself. Its 150-year-old, 30-foot stone arch is still intact, but is not easy to see.

The **Warren Mill,** now a private home, was part of Nicholas's commercial complex at the canal lock. It is behind the fence and is easily seen from the culvert.

You can reach the river by continuing over the tracks about a quarter of a mile on the gravel road. No sign of the would-be port remains, but the sight of the James, flowing strongly between close banks and around great river rocks, is grand.

Return to the junction of Warren Road and James River Road and turn left at the stop sign. The James River Road follows SR 627, then 626/627 and then 626. Keep bearing left.

About two and a half miles from the stop sign at Warren Road, on the left, is the **historical marker** for the site of the first Episcopal church in Albemarle, Ballenger Church of St. Anne's parish. It vanished after the Revolution.

In another four and a half miles you will reach **Howardsville,** the southernmost settlement in Albemarle, at the confluence of the James and the **Rockfish** rivers. It is named for one of Albemarle's first court justices.

> This section of the James River Road follows the 1832 Howardsville Turnpike, established as a link to the Staunton-James River Turnpike when Howardsville was a tobacco inspection station.

> The canal crossed the Rockfish on an aqueduct—a wooden trough supported by stone piers. The piers can be easily seen, having been incorporated into the supports for the railroad bridge.

Cross the Rockfish into Nelson County and take the first left (SR 602) to cross over the James. The confluence of the rivers that form the southern edge of the county can be seen from the bridge. Turn around at the first opportunity to return.

> One of the founders of Albemarle, William Cabell, was an assistant surveyor who plunged into the uncharted territory

south of what is now Howardsville to make extensive land acquisitions. His plantation, Warminster, was about four miles up the James from here. Once it was in Albemarle; now it is in Nelson County.

Cabell, along with Peter Jefferson, Joshua Fry and Thomas Walker, was one of the first members of the court that governed the county. This multi-talented justice was also a physician, ferry operator, storekeeper, explorer and trader.

Back across the Rockfish in Howardsville, turn left on the Howardsville Turnpike (SR 602).

The two oldest buildings that survive in the village stand high on a bank where the road jogs left. They are so close together that they almost seem one building.

The **Howardsville Methodist Church** (1851) is a temple form with white pilasters. This is the most unchanged of the antebellum Methodist churches in Albemarle. It has the original pews, floors and light fixtures. In 1983 the congregation merged with others and no longer uses the sanctuary for worship service. The building beside it is the **Masonic temple.**

A little over a half mile from the church is **Monticola,** a house that enjoys both state and national landmark status and is open for tours by appointment.

The original brick home was built in 1853 by Howardsville banker D.J. Hartsook on land acquired through his wife's family, the Cabells and Carringtons. Around 1900 the Greek revival style was enhanced with the four 25-foot columns salvaged from the Exchange Hotel in Richmond.

In 1940 D.W. Griffith, the legendary filmmaker ("Birth of a Nation"), rented Monticola from its then owner, Miss Emily

Nolting, spinster daughter of a U.S. ambassador to Belgium. The place appealed to Griffith because it was so run down and still lacked indoor plumbing and electricity. He paid the large rental fee well ahead of the scheduled filming, and when the crew returned they found Miss Nolting had used the money for painting, landscaping, etc. He had to remove all improvements before filming could begin.

The movie in question was "Virginia," starring Fred MacMurray, Madeleine Carroll and Sterling Hayden.

Continue northward on the Howardsville Turnpike, a pleasant drive along the beautiful Rockfish, one of Virginia's Scenic Rivers, about five mile to the junction with Schuyler Road (SR 800). Turn left to visit **Schuyler,** the Nelson County birthplace and boyhood home of writer Earl Hamner.

Appleberry Mountain, alias Walton's Mountain, stands guard over the town.

William Appleberry, who owned 5,000 acres on this mountain, opposed slavery and hired freedmen to work his fields. During the Revolution, he offered refuge and 25 acres to Hessian prisoners of war who escaped from The Barracks. Several came.

As the road winds into Schuyler, it passes the soapstone works, a surprising pocket of industry in a forested mountain cove.

Schuyler's seam of soapstone, unlike the abandoned quarry at Alberene, is still mined and the stone is processed here.

Past the stoneworks and over a ridge the road winds into the heart of Schuyler, which seems nearly untouched since John Boy's Depression boyhood.

Turn left at the stop sign at SR 617, follow it past the church and homes, then turn right on SR 693 to cross the bridge at the dramatic old **hydroelectric dam** on the Rockfish. Drive on a little way to see more of the homes, many of them build in the 1920s from prefabricated kits ordered from the Sears Roebuck catalog, then retrace your path back into Schuyler.

Don't turn at the junction with Schuyler Road (back to the soapstone plant), but continue straight on SR 617. The **Hamner home,** a private residence still in the family, is the first house on the left, behind the chain link fence.

Just beyond the house, up the hill and past the modern post office, is the old Schuyler Elementary School, now the **Walton's Mountain Museum.**

> The museum offers replicas of sets used in the television program, including Ike Godsey's store, a collection of original scripts and other memorabilia related to the fictional Walton family.

This ends Tour 11. To return to Charlottesville by the most direct route, take Schuyler road back past the stoneworks to Irish Road (VA 6) and turn left to reach US 29, about five miles. This four lane divided highway will take you back to Charlottesville.

Or, if you want to experience the wild beauty of the Rockfish River and drive through the rugged hills and steep mountain slopes that were the childhood playground and training grounds of Confederate raider John Singleton Mosby, take SR 617 to US 29, about 9.5 miles.

> Mosby was born at Edgerton, Virginia, in 1833. After his birth the family moved to a home nearer Charlottesville, about four miles south of town on the Old Lynchburg Road (SR 631).

Mosby was the leader of a small band of hard-riding partisans (never more than a few hundred men) who continually routed federal cavalry, destroyed communications, appropriated supplies and were, in general, a great nuisance to the Army of the Potomac in northern Virginia. Protected by the people of the region, which came to be known as "Mosby's Confederacy," the rangers eluded the strong forces sent to capture them and were active throughout the war.

Although Mosby did little fighting in Albemarle, he happened to be on furlough and having a shave in a barber shop in Charlottesville when Union generals Sheridan and Custer came through. The lad holding his horse warned him of their impending arrival, and the agile Mosby, his face covered with lather, leaped upon his horse and threw the boy a silver dollar before even learning where the danger lay. To his chagrin, he rode right into a contingent of the astonished Yankees, but jumped a barricade and escaped down Park Street.

Mosby's Rangers were active throughout the war and were finally disbanded on April 21, 1865, in Clarke County, Virginia. Mosby died in 1916.

About four miles past Schuyler, bear right at the junction with SR 639 to stay on 617 through the mountain community of **Rockfish.** It is about 5.5 miles from Rockfish to US 29.

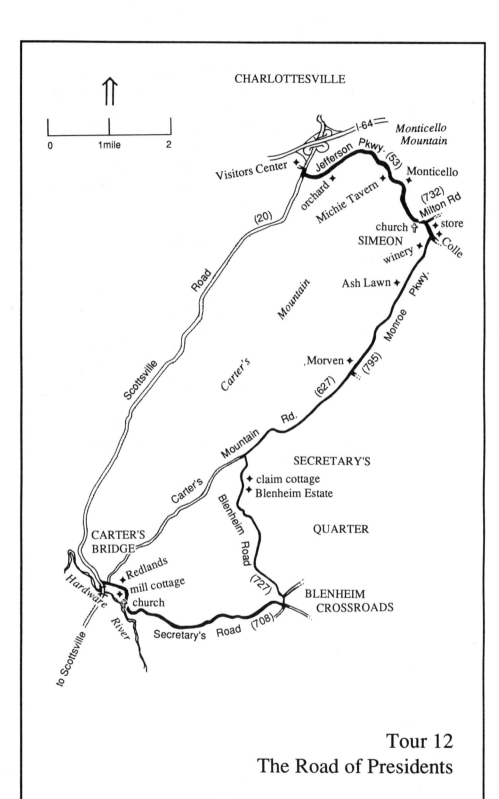

CHARLOTTESVILLE

I-64

Monticello Mountain

Visitors Center

Jefferson Pkwy. (53)

Monticello

orchard

(732)

Michie Tavern

Milton Rd

(20)

church ✝

store

SIMEON

Colle

winery

Ash Lawn

Mountain

Monroe Pkwy.

Scottsville

Road

Carter's

Morven

(795)

(627)

Mountain

Rd.

SECRETARY'S

Carter's

claim cottage
Blenheim Estate

QUARTER

CARTER'S
BRIDGE

Blenheim Road

Redlands

(727)

mill cottage

BLENHEIM
CROSSROADS

Hardware

church

to Scottsville

River

Secretary's Road (708)

0   1mile   2

Tour 12
The Road of Presidents

Tour 12　　　　　The Road of Presidents

Michie Tavern to Carter's Bridge: 14 miles

As this tour explores the east side of Carter's Mountain, it passes Monticello and Ash Lawn-Highland, the homes of presidents Thomas Jefferson and James Monroe, other early plantations that today are elegant estates and working farms.

From the Visitors Center, turn right onto Scottsville Road (VA 20), then turn left in 100 yards onto the Thomas Jefferson Parkway (VA 53).

> This road has been used by pilgrims since the 1920s, when Monticello was opened to the public, but Jefferson used a road that curved around and up his little mountain from Secretary's Ford on the Rivanna River.

> In the early days of settlement, the passage between **Monticello Mountain** and the Great or **Carter's Mountain** was known as **Thoroughfare Gap.**

About a mile along the parkway you will see the entrance to **Carter's Mountain Orchard.** The road up to the orchard is steep and narrow.

> In the fall you can pick your own apples (several varieties), and at the same time enjoy a spectacular view both east and west.

A few hundred yards past the orchard entrance is **Michie Tavern,** centered in a cluster of buildings hugging the mountain side.

The double-porched tavern was built about 1784 in the north-west part of the county by John Michie, a Scottish immigrant. Moved here in 1927, the tavern offers a buffet luncheon daily as well as tours that tell of tavern life and the Michie family.

The 1797 mill was moved here from Meadow Run Creek in Augusta County in the Shenandoah Valley. It houses a gift shop.

It is a half mile through shady forest on a very curvy road from the tavern to the entrance to **Monticello.** In the parking area you will find information, a shuttle bus to the house and a shop that sells plants popular in the 18th century. This is but an introduction to "Jefferson Country."

Monticello is the manifestation of Thomas Jefferson's creative mind. So full of inventions, experiments and design is this magnificent plantation that repeat visits reveal ever more. Jefferson began his house in 1770 on property he inherited from this father and kept right on building until near his death in 1826. Through the restoration of house and grounds, it is coming ever closer to Jefferson's plan.

Jefferson experimented with classical architectural motifs, often adapted from the designs of Italian architect Palladio, but he also added devices to improve efficiency, such as triple-sashed windows and skylights, and he substituted local materials to save costs. Studying Jefferson's manipulation of his material world at Monticello helps us understand how he used the ideas of Enlightenment to devise a democratic and flexible government.

A mile and three tenths past Monticello is the junction with Milton Road (SR 732), the road to Jefferson's **Tufton** farm and his lands near Milton.

At this junction is a crossroads community called **Simeon.**

On the left is a store that offers elegant picnic supplies, including local wines and other products made in Virginia.

Across from the store is **St. Luke's Episcopal Chapel.**

Established in 1892, this chapel was one of three mountain missions sponsored by the Christ Episcopal Church in Charlottesville. The wooden mother church was replaced by a stone building in 1898, and some of its lumber was used in the construction of this chapel.

Beyond the store and adjacent to it is **Colle** (meaning "hill" in Italian), once Filippo Mazzei's vineyard and home.

Mazzei, a Tuscan-born physician and London wine merchant, wanted to start a wine industry in America. Jefferson found this an idea totally compatible with his own horticultural interests, encourage Mazzei to settle next to Monticello and gave him some land to enlarge his farm.

Just as the first grapes were ready for harvest, Mazzei was chosen to serve as America's agent in Europe for the purchase of supplies for the Revolution. In Mazzei's absence, Colle was rented to Baron von Riedesel, the Hessian officer whose troops were imprisoned at The Barracks. The baron's horses ran amok in the vineyard, trampling and destroying several years of work. Winemaking was never revived at Colle in Mazzei's time.

Across the road, just past the chapel, is the entrance to the **Simeon Winery,** built on some of Colle's original fields.

Since 1981 wines have been made here following Tuscan methods, under the supervision of a Tuscan winemaster.

Bear right in a mile and a half on the Monroe Parkway (SR 795) to **Ash Lawn-Highland.**

James Monroe called this plantation Highland with a nod to his Scottish ancestors. The Monroes moved here on November 23, 1799. Jefferson wooed his younger political colleague to his neighborhood and supervised the building of the house while Monroe served as minister to France.

Part of the original house (painted soft yellow) survives; a later owner added a taller wing to replace a part that burned. Though the house is a modest one, it is filled with Monroe possessions, including some formal Napoleonic furniture. Monroe and his family were thorough Francophiles.

There are tours daily; the guides bring the family, often overshadowed by Jefferson, to life. An outdoor music festival is held in the summer.

The next farm south of Ash Lawn-Highland is **Morven** (Scottish for "ridge of hills"). The house, a Virginia Historic Landmark, cannot be seen from the road, but the area has an interesting history.

The Morven lands were first known as Indian Camp for the Monacan settlement here. The first English owner (circa 1730) was Secretary John Carter. Colonel William Short, minister to the Netherlands and later to Spain, acquired 500 acres here in 1795 with some assistance from Jefferson. The 1820 house was built by a friend of Jefferson named Higginbotham; the carpenter was Martin Thacker, one of Jefferson's skilled workmen.

In the 1960s Mr. and Mrs. Charles A. Stone revived Morven as a horse farm. Their horse Shuvee, winner of the Filly Triple Crown and the Alabama Stakes, was the first mare to win the Jockey Club Gold Cup and become a member of the Racing Hall of Fame. She was one of several famous horses foaled here.

The Stones created a fabulous garden that became a regular stop on the Albemarle Garden Week Tour, which otherwise features different gardens each year. The current owner expanded the gardens and continues this tradition of hospitality.

Where Monroe Parkway makes a ninety-degree turn to the left, follow the Morven fence straight onto Carter's Mountain Road (SR 627). Over the next four miles the road passes through rolling fields that were important horse farms in the 19th century.

One of those farms, **Ellerslie,** was cut from Morven's lands in 1842 and was owned by John O. Harris. Harris's daughter, Thomasia, met Richard J. Hancock of Alabama, a Confederate soldier convalescing in Albemarle. They married after the war and built Ellerslie into a great power that influenced the world of horse racing for half a century.

Turn left onto Blenheim Road (SR 727). In half a mile begins the fence of **Blenheim Estate,** Secretary Carter's first plantation, now a Virginia Historic Landmark.

Look across the bowl-like depression in the field to see the Blenheim **claim cottage.** The mansion is just beyond.

Although John Carter never lived here, he supplied the farm with the requisite claim cottage and brought in slaves to clear the land. His son Edward, who represented Albemarle in the House of Burgesses 1767-69 and in the state House of Delegates in 1788, made Blenheim his principal home.

Andrew Stevenson, a congressman, speaker of the House of Representatives and minister to England, lived here 1836-57.

His wife, Sally Coles of nearby Enniscorthy, was a great beauty with strong ties to her home. When her husband was ambassador to England, she gave Albemarle pippin apples to Queen Victoria, much to the queen's liking.

Blenheim Road was one of Secretary Carter's rolling roads and passes through was called **Secretary's Quarter** as it goes toward **Blenheim Crossroads,** about two and a half miles from the estate.

A "quarter" was 400 acres of land, an old English division of property. Slaves were assigned to certain quarters, and the term eventually came to mean a place where one lives or bunks.

At the stop sign in Blenheim Crossroads, turn right on Martin King's Road (SR 708). In about two and a half miles, on the left, is the historical marker for the **Forge Church,** now vanished.

The church was named for Carter's nearby forge. After the Boston tea party, the church was the meeting spot for community leaders who gathered to show support for the ideals that were to evolve into revolution.

Just past the marker, around the curve, is the original miller's cottage for **Secretary's Mill** on the banks of the Hardware River.

Beyond the cottage, on the right, is the entrance to **Redlands,** a plantation still in the Carter family.

The house cannot be seen from here, but is can be seen from a distance at the junction of the Scottsville Road (VA 20) and Fry's Path (SR 627), the beginning of Tour 13.

Redlands is a survivor of John Carter's original grant. When Carter's grandson Robert married Polly Coles from the nearby Green Mountain, her father built the mansion for them. Martin Thacker began the building in 1798.

Turn left at the stop sign beyond Redlands to reach the Scottsville Road at Carter's Bridge. The guided portion of the tour ends here.

You may return directly to Charlottesville via the Scottsville Road is you turn right at Carter's Bridge. Or, turn left on the Scottsville Road a half mile to the junction with Fry's Path, the beginning of Tour 13, the Green Mountain.

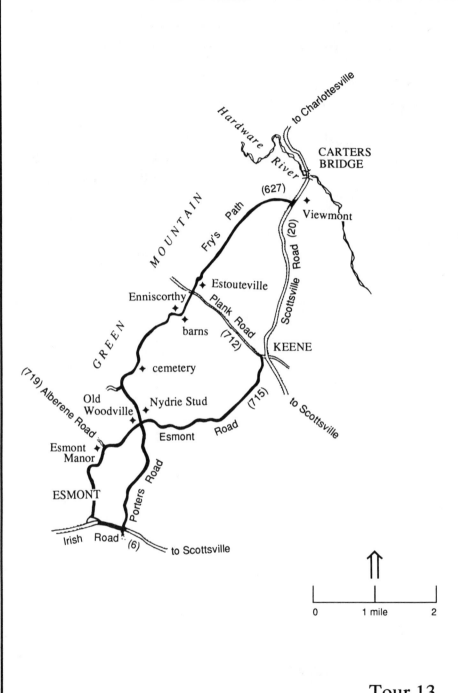

to Charlottesville

Hardware River

CARTERS
BRIDGE

(627)

Viewmont

M O U N T A I N

Fry's Path

Estouteville

Enniscorthy

Plank Road (712)

barns

Scottsville Road (20)

KEENE

G R E E N

cemetery

(719) Alberene Road

Old
Woodville

Nydrie Stud

Road (715)

to Scottsville

Esmont

Esmont
Manor

ESMONT

Porters Road

Irish Road (6)   to Scottsville

0   1 mile   2

Tour 13
On Green Mountain

Tour 13 On Green Mountain

*Green Mountain Ridge from Viewmont to
Esmont: 8 miles*

This tour is an encounter with nature on Green Mountain, the
southernmost ridge of the Southwest Mountains. Its hidden gems
of high civilization are three historic homes built by a single pioneering family and a thoroughbred horse farm added by another.

Begin this tour at the junction of the Scottsville Road (VA 20) and
Fry's Path (SR 627), nine miles south of the Visitors Center—
just past Carter's Bridge. Tour 10 describes the sights between the
Visitors Center and this junction.

Turn right on Fry's Path. The road is narrow and unpaved but well
graded and easily driven.

> Joshua Fry cut the road from his Viewmont farm (on the east
> side of the Scottsville Road at the junction) to connect with
> the farm roads atop the mountain.

> In this section are groves of regal tulip poplar trees, some of
> them 200 feet tall, that form a botanical cathedral with occa-
> sional windows to the Blue Ridge. Generations of these trees
> preceded white settlement. They bud before all other trees in
> the spring and produce pale green and yellow tulip-shaped
> flowers. The leaves mist the slopes with a fresh, clear color-
> that gave Green Mountain its name.

So uncultivated is this narrow forest path that you may wonder if
nature has swallowed all signs of man. Then, 1.6 miles along, a

brick-columned gate signals the back entrance of the **Estouteville** plantation. Drive well beyond the gate and look back to the left for the best view of the house.

Hope of finding substantial deposits of iron ore, plus its proximity to the James River wharves, lured John Coles I to purchase 3,000 acres here between 1740 and 1747. The Irish-born tobacco merchant from Richmond never lived here himself, but his descendants, successful merchant-tobacco planters, established four plantations along the ridge.

Estouteville, considered by many to be the most beautiful home in Albemarle, is certainly the most beautiful of the three Coles houses you will see.

John Coles III (grandson of John I) and his wife, Selina Skipwith, built Estouteville between 1827 and 1830. It is near the site of a much earlier and smaller Coles house called Calycanthus Hill for a shrub with a sweet-smelling woody flower which grew in profusion here.

Selina was a daughter of Sir Peyton Skipwith, Virginia's only English baronet. Her mother, Jean Miller Skipwith, was an intellectual famous for her library and garden at Prestwould, the family estate near Clarksville in Mecklenburg County. Selina honored an ancestor, a French nobleman, when she selected the name of her new home.

Philadelphian James Dinsmore, a master builder trained by Jefferson, gave Estouteville the graceful Tuscan porticos. Jefferson's influence is apparent in the wedding of Palladian elements and American materials.

Look to the right as the road curves around Estouteville to share its fine view of the Ragged Mountains and the Blue Ridge.

Fry's Path ends at the stop sign, its junction with Plank Road (SR 712), the old Staunton-James River Turnpike.

Cross the intersection and continue south on the Green Mountain Road (still SR 627), which had its beginnings as a tobacco rolling road.

Less than a half mile from the junction, at a 90-degree right turn on the **Enniscorthy** plantation, stand a small log barn and a larger one with a silo.

> The smaller barn was built by Isaac Coles, son of John Coles II, about 1815. For a barn to survive this long attests to its excellent construction—notice its unusually fine detailing. This structure has beaded siding above the logs and boxed cornices. Slaves threshed the wheat on the main floor; the clean grain dropped onto a conveyor belt below the floor grate.

The road turns sharply to the west as it passes the barns. Where it turns south again, look to the right, through the gate, to see the 1850 Enniscorthy manor house, the third built on this site.

> The first of three houses called Enniscorthy was named by John Coles II for his father's birthplace near Leinster, Ireland. John II added to his father's initial land purchase, amassing over 9,000 acres in all. He raised tobacco, corn and wheat that was processed in his own mill, and operated a general merchandise store at the river town of Howardsville.
>
> John II was a soldier in the Revolution, a colonel of the militia and commander of the troops guarding the prisoners of war held at The Barracks. Governor Jefferson and his family escaped capture by the British in June 1781 by taking shelter among the Coles family at Enniscorthy.

Isaac Coles served as Jefferson's secretary, a sort of chief of staff, during the President's second term and was an officer in the War of 1812. He returned to Enniscorthy in middle age when he edged out Daniel Webster in a bid for the hand of Julianna Stricker Rankin, the widow of Christopher Rankin, a U.S. Congressman from Mississippi.

Isaac and Julianna built a grander house on the foundation of the original. Jefferson's builder, William B. Phillips, did the brickwork at the same time he was working on Christ Church at Glendower. Burwell, one of the slaves Jefferson freed by his will and one of the most skilled of his artisans, painted the house. Enniscorthy II burned in 1839.

The house you see today was built by the widowed Julianna in 1850. Though not as illustrious in its architecture as Enniscorthy II, it served Coles families until 1925.

A third Coles plantation, Tallwood, is near Enniscorthy but cannot be seen from the road.

Tucker Coles, another son of John II, built Tallwood 1804-1834. He married Helen Skipwith, the sister of Selina Skipwith Coles of Estoutville. Helen described her husband's house as "so small it had no name," when she arrived as a bride. With a fortune inherited from her mother, Helen greatly improved Tallwood.

Around 1840, a party of Native Americans obtained permission to visit a burial mound on the Tallwood property and to camp nearby. They were observed in ceremonial dances honoring their dead, the last such ritual seen in Albemarle.

On past Enniscorthy is the private cemetery of the Van Clief family, horse breeders of **Nydrie Farms.** The entrance is six tenths of a mile from the cemetery.

Nydrie is a world-reknowned thoroughbred stud farm operated by the third generation of the Van Clief family. Daniel Van Clief, a member of the Virginia House of Delegates, inherited Nydrie from his parents in the 1940s. He produced the world's most sought-after sire, Kentucky Derby winner Northern Dancer. Jet Pilot, another Derby winner, was bred here, and Natalma, Northern Dancer's dam, was bred, foaled and raised at Nydrie.

The 1891 mammoth mansion with its 64 rooms proved to be too much for the Van Cliefs, who moved to more humanly proportioned quarters. Of Nydrie's original late 19th-century buildings only the brick Gothic stables remain today. The horses look over their doors to a charming cobbled courtyard enhanced by ivy covered walls.

Young interns learning equine management offer informal tours to visitors 10 a.m. to 3 p.m., Monday through Saturday.

A few yards south of Nydrie's entrance is **Old Woodville,** the oldest of the Coles family homes on the mountain.

John Coles II built the central square of this 1794-96 house for his eldest son, Walter. Its architecture is that of the early settlement of Albemarle, uninfluenced by Jefferson's classic revival.

John Fortune, a free black neighbor, sawed most of the wood for the construction of the house. William Walker, a miller on the Hardware River, provided additional lumber. William Bates, a skilled local carpenter, directed the slaves who built the house.

Just south of Old Woodville is the intersection with Esmont Road (SR 715). Turn right.

In just under a mile, turn right on Alberene Road (SR 719) and go just a tenth of a mile to see the **Esmont estate,** a Virginia Historic Landmark.

> A square brick building outlined with white, the house was built between 1816 and 1820 for Dr. Charles Cocke. Esmont's Doric entablatures reflect Jefferson's classic revival influence, though there is no evidence of his direct involvement in the design.

> In the 1970s, Esmont was owned by Roger McBride, who twice was the Libertarian Party's presidential candidate. As executor of Laura Ingalls Wilder's estate, he granted Michael Landon the rights to produce the "Little House on the Prairie" TV series.

Turn around and return to Esmont Road. Turn right and go about a mile to visit the **village of Esmont,** a half-mile-long string of buildings.

> The late 19th-century village, which took its name from the estate, developed when the Nelson and Albemarle Railway ran a spur line to the soapstone quarry at Alberene. Workers who lived along the line commuted to work. Passenger service ended in 1950 and the town declined, but it still has vestiges of its depot boom time.

To return to Charlottesville, turn left onto Pace's Store Road (SR 753) at the stop sign at the south end of village. Turn left again onto Irish Road (VA 6).

In 3.7 miles, turn left on Buck Langhorne Road (SR 626), which will take you to the Scottsville Road (VA 20). Turn left (north) to Charlottesville.

Court Square, Main Street and the University:
8 miles

Court Square and its surrounds mark the political center of the Charlottesville. The University of Virginia, to the west, is its academic center. Between the two lies the historic commercial district, the meeting ground 'twixt town and gown.

You may want to read this chapter before you drive it. Parking is scarce, and the tour notes only sights that can be seen from your automobile. The Visitors Center has walking tour maps.

From the Visitors Center, drive north on the Scottsville Road and Monticello Avenue (VA 20) about two miles to its intersection with Jefferson Street, one block past the traffic signal at Market. Turn left on Jefferson.

At the end of the first block (8th Street NE), on the left, stands Charlottesville's most elegant federal town house, the three-story **Carter-Gilmer House** (1830).

> Dr. Charles Gilmer of Pen Park built the house with a separate office to accommodate his family and his medical practice. Gilmer's younger brother, Francis, a brilliant scholar, was recruited for the university's first faculty as Jefferson's agent in Europe.

Continue one block to 7th Street NE and look to the left, but don't turn. On the right (west) side of the street, in the middle of the block, is the **Molyneux House,** a story-and-a-half, with a tin roof.

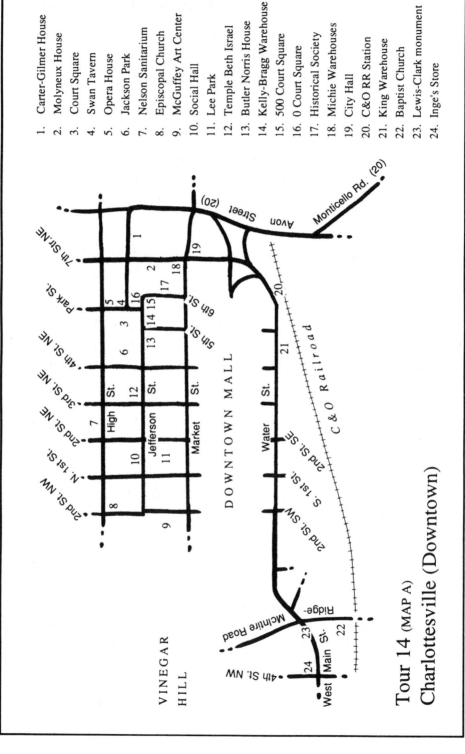

1. Carter-Gilmer House
2. Molyneux House
3. Court Square
4. Swan Tavern
5. Opera House
6. Jackson Park
7. Nelson Sanitarium
8. Episcopal Church
9. McGuffey Art Center
10. Social Hall
11. Lee Park
12. Temple Beth Israel
13. Butler Norris House
14. Kelly-Bragg Warehouse
15. 500 Court Square
16. 0 Court Square
17. Historical Society
18. Michie Warehouses
19. City Hall
20. C&O RR Station
21. King Warehouse
22. Baptist Church
23. Lewis-Clark monument
24. Inge's Store

Tour 14 (MAP A)
Charlottesville (Downtown)

This is a very early structure that originally stood in the town of Milton. When Milton declined as a trade center, a few of its houses were moved to locations in and around Charlottesville.

Cross 7th and proceed one block to Park Street. You will be facing **Court Square.**

The court house stands at the center of the original bounds of Charlottesville, named for King George III's young queen. The town site, near the Secretary's Ford and the commercial center at Milton, consisted of only a few mills and a scattering of farms when it was designated the county seat in 1761.

Richard Randolph owned the 1,000 acres upon which the town center was laid out. The boundaries were McIntire Road (Vinegar Hill) on the west and 9th Street on the east; residential High Street was the northern boundary and commercial Water Street the southern.

The brick building on the right houses the private **Red Land Club.** This was the site of the **Swan Tavern** in colonial days.

The Swan was owned by John Jouett, a French Huguenot who served in the Virginia House of Burgesses. The building you see here is not the original; it collapsed in 1828.

On June 4, 1781, John's son Jack, in a daring, all-night ride, effectively warned Governor Jefferson (at Monticello) and members of the Virginia Assembly (most of whom were staying at this and other nearby taverns) that Col. Tarleton and his dragoons were closing in on them. Daniel Boone, one of the few legislators captured, was released the next day.

Turn right on Park Street and look at the north end of the court-house, the part that backs up to High Street.

This section is all that remains of the second courthouse (1803), which was probably designed by Jefferson. It was remodelled in 1859, 1896 and 1938; the bricks were covered with stucco and painted.

The original courthouse, a wooden one, was built in 1762. Various religious denominations used the courtroom in rotation until church buildings were erected. Jefferson liked the communal approach and remembered it as a period of toleration. Not to be too forgiving, the grounds held the punishment tools of pillory, stocks and whipping post.

The building on the right, facing the courthouse at Park and High, is the **Levy Opera House,** built in 1851 as a town hall.

This Greek Revival building was named for Commodore Uriah Levy, who bought Monticello in 1836 and began restoring it. The opera house presented traveling minstrel shows and great artists, including Sarah Bernhardt. During the Civil War it was a Confederate foundry.

Turn left on High Street. As you pass the courthouse, note the statue of Stonewall Jackson in **Jackson Park.**

Sculptor Charles Keck completed the great equestrian monument in 1921. It depicts a bare-headed Jackson riding at considerable speed on his favorite mount, Little Sorrel.

Between 3rd Street NE and 2nd Street NE, note the double-porched brick house on the right, now used as offices.

This was the 1887 home of Dr. Hugh Nelson, Jr., who used the 1830 house on the corner as his sanitarium 1895-1902.

Continue on High Street two blocks and turn left on 2nd Street NW. **Christ Episcopal Church** is on the corner.

This Gothic stone church with its Tiffany windows is the second building on this site, replacing an 1824 Jefferson design.

From Christ Church, look ahead to the **McGuffey Art Center,** once an elementary school, on the right.

The school was named for William Holmes McGuffey, author of the *McGuffey Readers,* used in schools all over the country well into the 20th century. His books had a profound moral effect on their young readers as well as creating a common curriculum for public school reading education. McGuffey, a professor of natural philosophy at the University of Virginia before and during the Civil War, championed public education—unsuccessfully in Charlottesville.

Turn left onto Jefferson Street.

In the middle of the second block on the left is **Social Hall,** built by John R. Jones. It is one of the oldest residences surviving in the downtown area.

Across from Social Hall is **Lee Park.**

The equestrian statue of Robert E. Lee was designed by H.M. Schrady, who died prior to its execution; Leo Lentelli completed it. It was unveiled in 1924 by Mary Walker Lee, the general's three-year-old granddaughter.

The statue was a gift of Paul Goodloe McIntire, who also built the now-replaced public library (on 2nd Street NE, across from the park) in 1919.

At 3rd Street NE and Jefferson is **Temple Beth Israel.**

This 1882 synagogue originally stood a block south of here. When the post office (now the Jefferson-Madison Main

Library) was built in 1903, the building was moved to this location, brick by brick.

On the right in the next two blocks are rows of early Charlottesville residences.

Directly across from Jackson Park and in the middle of the block (410 East Jefferson) is the **Butler-Norris House.**

Edward Butler, a signer of the Albemarle resolution for independence, built the west portion around 1785. It is the only 18th-century building on Court Square. John Kelly, a university building contractor, owned it in 1808.

The Butler house is connected to the Norris house by the bricks in the second floor. Opie Norris, Kelly's son-in-law, and an active principal in the building of the Rockfish Gap Turnpike, built the house and shop.

On the corner of 5th Street NE and Jefferson is the 1826 **Kelly-Bragg Warehouse.**

This dry goods, confectioner, grocery and liquor store was built by James Kelly. The formal entrance was added in 1921.

Continue on Jefferson Street and cross 5th Street NE.

The land beneath **500 Court Square** was once owned by Dr. Thomas Walker of Castle Hill on the Old Mountain Road.

Before 1791 this was the location of the Eagle Tavern. The first local hotel (successor to the tavern) was the Farish House, the leading hotel in 1854. It has been rebuilt many times; in this century it was the Hotel Colonial and then the Monticello Hotel before it became 500 Court Square.

Diagonally across Jefferson is **Nothing Court Square.** Reserved as a horse lot, it was given the number 0 on the original town plan.

The building dates at least to 1829. The ghost of a sign on the south wall reads "Benson and Bro. Auction Rooms." It is believed the company dealt in slaves.

Turn right (south) on 6th Street NE.

The row building on the left dates to the mid 19th century. Monsieur Lescot, a Swiss watchmaker and spirits seller, and the miserly Johnny Yergain, a saddlemaker, kept shops here.

The single-story building at the end was the law office of U.S. Senator Thomas Martin from 1900 to 1922. Martin, a Scottsville native, was the majority leader of the U.S. Senate (1912-19). He won his seat in 1893 in a hot contest with Robert E. Lee's nephew, Fitzhugh Lee.

Turn left onto Market Street and get into the right lane so you can turn right onto 7th Street NE at the traffic signal. The **Michie Company** warehouses and **City Hall** are at the turn.

The Michie Company publishes the law codes for various states; they are stored here.

In one block the street curves to the right and merges with Water Street. In front of you is the 1904 **C&O station,** an elegant beaux arts design, now home to retail shops.

The Louisa Railroad arrived here in 1848. As the Virginia Central and later the Chesapeake and Ohio, it linked Charlottesville to points east and west. The area near the tracks had many warehouses, liveries and other commercial buildings. Some are very well preserved. The **King Warehouse** (c. 1915) is on the left, just past the train station.

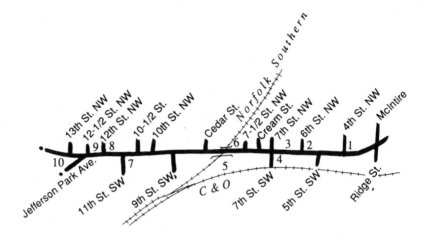

1. Inge's
2. Paxton Place
3. Gleason's Hotel
4. Baptist Church
5. Amtrak Station
6. Starr Hill stores
7. Patton Mansion (bank)
8. Vowles House
9. Livers House
10. Clark statue

Tour 14 (MAP B)
Charlottesville (Main Street)

Water Street bends to the left and ends at the traffic signal at the top of the hill several blocks ahead. Stay in the center lanes to go straight onto Main Street.

As you cross the intersection, glance left to see the 1884 **Mount Zion Baptist Church,** a Virginia Historic Landmark.

> This church takes a strong position in civic leadership and is an important meeting place for community activists; Jesse Jackson and Jimmy Carter are among the many famous visitors who have spoken in the beautiful sanctuary with its Tiffany windows.

You are on the crest of **Vinegar Hill,** made famous in the University of Virginia fight song, "From Vinegar Hill to Rugby Road, we're going to get drunk tonight. . . . "

> The **monument** in the center of the intersection commemorates two of Albemarle's native sons, Meriwether Lewis and William Clark, leaders of the expedition that charted the Louisiana Purchase, and Sacajawea, their Shoshone guide.
>
> The Vinegar Hill neighborhood is bounded by McIntire, Main, Preston and 4th Street NW. This black community of about 20 acres was run down, but still a viable and yeasty business and social center, when the city's urban renewal enthusiasm decided it must be rehabilitated in the 1950s. Most of the buildings were razed in 1963, but the rehabilitation bogged down until 1983.
>
> During the civil rights skirmishes that closed Charlottesville's public schools in the 1960s, Vinegar Hill stood as a bleak reminder of the dispersal of the black community.

The building at Main and 4th Street NW once was **Inge's Store,** the only Vinegar Hill business active into the mid 1970s.

This was originally the Johnson W. Pitts House, built about 1820. G.F. Inge established his grocery store and residence here in the 1890s in what was a Methodist parsonage.

As you head toward the university a mile away, you will pass several federal period buildings along this stretch of Main Street, once a part of the Three Notched Road.

At 503 West Main is the 1824 **Paxton Place,** built by J.D. Paxton, a Presbyterian minister. It once stood on 33 acres.

In the next block is the columned **Gleason's Hotel** (later called the Albemarle Hotel), the oldest surviving local hotel. It was active until the turn of the century.

At the corner of 7th Street SW, on the left, is the **First Baptist Church,** built on the site of the Mudwall School, which served as a hospital during the Civil War.

Judge R.T.W. Duke, Jr., son of the Confederate colonel, recalled that as a small boy he was shocked at the surgeons' indifference as they tossed amputated limbs onto the garbage heap beside the hospital after the second battle of Manassas.

Past the church and below the level of Main Street is the **Southern Railroad station,** now used by Amtrak.

The line linking Orange Courthouse and Charlottesville opened in 1863, and the station was built soon after. This railroad operated at various times as the Orange and Alexandria, the Washington City, the Virginia Midland and Great Southern and the Richmond and Danville.

Across from the station is a row of old stores, collectively called **Starr Hill,** the remnants of a commercial district that grew up around the railroad depot.

Continue down Main Street. The bank on the left, between 10th and 11th streets SW, was once the **Patton Mansion,** circa 1845.

At 12th Street NW, on the right, stands the **Vowles House,** which is actually a combination of two houses.

Its earliest recorded owner was James Dinsmore, Jefferson's gifted carpenter. The house that makes up the eastern part of the residence was built in 1824, the western one in 1839.

The handsome brick house at the corner of 12-1/2 Street NW is the 1820s **Livers House,** one of the finest federal-style buildings in the city.

The **University of Virginia** was located outside of town when it opened in 1826. The town grew toward the university, and the houses you passed were built in the years following.

At Main and Jefferson Park Avenue, on the left, is the **statue of George Rogers Clark** in a small, wooded park. Bear right on University Avenue, a continuation of the old Three Notched Road.

Just beyond the railroad overpass, on the left, are the buildings of the University of Virginia **medical school.** On the right are the **Corner Shops,** historic buildings with up-to-date businesses catering to student needs.

On the left in a few hundred yards, set back from the road atop a low hill, is the jewel of the University Grounds, the **Rotunda.**

Modeled on the Roman Pantheon, this was the heart of Jefferson's academical village. It was begun in 1822, Jefferson's 79th year, and was completed five years later, shortly after his death. Free tours are available.

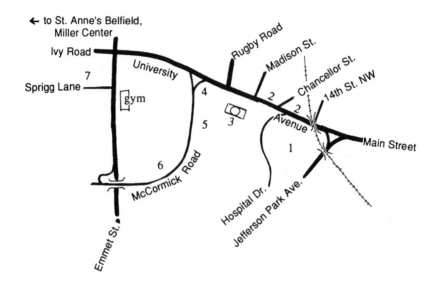

1. Medical School
2. Corner Shops
3. Rotunda
4. Chapel
5. Ranges
6. Monroe Hill
7. Morea

Tour 14 (MAP C)
Charlottesville (University)

Just past the Rotunda, turn left on McCormick Road. At the corner is the **University Chapel,** scene of many student weddings.

On the left and right are the **Ranges,** the single-story brick quarters of honor students, who deem it a privilege to live here, even though their communal bathrooms are only accessible from the outside.

> Edgar Allan Poe's room was Number 13, on the near end; Woodrow Wilson's was Number 28, at the far end.

Beyond the Ranges, around a curve on the right, is **Monroe Hill** (ca. 1790), once the main house on one of James Monroe's farms.

> Monroe held almost 30 acres here until he moved to Ash Lawn-Highland in 1799. It was this property, with an additional tract, that became the Grounds of the university.

McCormick road is not always open to through traffic. If you can, continue across the bridge and turn right, then left, onto Emmet Street (US 29). In a long block, past the Memorial Gym, turn left on Sprigg Lane.

[If McCormick is blocked, go back to University Avenue and turn left. Turn left again at Emmet Street, then right on Sprigg Lane.]

Behind the brick dorms on the right is **Morea** (1834), one of the first houses built for a university professor outside the academic village on the Lawn.

> John Patten Emmet, professor of natural history on the first faculty, designed his home and named it for the *Morus Multi-caulis* mulberry, his hope for the establishment of a local silk industry. His lawn was a living botany laboratory that included varieties of peonies, grapes and 150 trees.

William Holding Echols, the professor for whom the university's Echols Scholars program is named, once lived here. The gifted Echols scholars enjoy full scholarships and devise their own programs of study.

The alumni gave Morea to the university in 1960; it was renovated in 1984 as a guest house for visiting professors.

Return to Emmet Street and turn left. Turn left again at the traffic signal at Ivy Road (US 250), a section of the old Three Notched Road.

St. Anne's Belfield School (K-12) is in a half mile, on the left.

The school began as the Albemarle Female Institute in 1857 and was continued after 1910 by the Episcopal church; in 1939 it moved to this 23-acre estate called Greenway Rise, once home to Elizabeth Bisland Wetmore, an early feminist.

At age 21 Ms. Wetmore, a journalist since age 17, was sponsored by the *New York Herald* in a race with Nellie Bly of the *New York World* in an attempt to beat Jules Verne's fictional trip around the world in 80 days. Bly won, but the undaunted Wetmore went on to become a successful biographer and travel writer. She died in 1929, having ended her days in Albemarle capped in lace, gowned by Worth, jewelled extravagantly, smoking incessantly and declaiming gloriously.

Lewis Mountain rises behind St. Anne's.

Brothers-in-law Joel Terrell and David Lewis patented 2,300 acres at the foot of this mountain, named for Lewis, in 1734.

Atop Lewis Mountain, but not visible from here, is the **Kearny Mansion,** sometimes mistaken for Monticello by visitors when they spot it from afar.

The Kearnys were Yankees, but they were comfortable in Albemarle because of Robert E. Lee's friendship with their kinsman. Gen. Stephen Watts Kearny died for the Union, but Lee personally saw that the body of his West Point classmate was returned to his family.

The Society of Precious Blood operated a monastic house of study and hospice here from the mid-1930s through World War II. It is now a private residence.

Bear right onto Old Ivy Road (SR 601) where the road forks at the traffic signal at the Exxon station to continue on the old Three Notched Road.

Immediately beyond the railroad overpass, turn right into the **Miller Center,** where the university has conducted studies of the American presidency since 1962, to see the **Lewis House.**

Jesse Pitman Lewis, a Revolutionary veteran and descendant of David Lewis, built two houses here in 1815; the first burned. The second was remodelled in 1855-56, then expanded in 1907 by U.S. Senator Thomas S. Martin, whose law offices we saw in Court Square.

The university has renamed the house in honor of William Faulkner, writer-in-residence at the university in the 1950s.

This completes the tour of Charlottesville. To get to the US 29 by-pass, turn right on Old Ivy Road. At the stop sign (a half mile), follow the signs.

Directory

Community Information

Albemarle County Planning and Community Development   804-296-5823
     401 McIntire, Charlottesville, VA 22902
Charlottesville-Albemarle Chamber of Commerce   804-295-3141
     5th and East Market Street, Charlottesville, VA 22902
Charlottesville-Albemarle Convention and Visitors Bureau   804-977-1783
     P.O. Box 161, Charlottesville, VA 22902
Charlottesville Economic Development   804-971-3110
     605 East Main Street, Charlottesville, VA 22901

General Information (Books, Maps, Conversation)

Albemarle County Historical Society   804-296-1492
     220 Court Square, Charlottesville, VA 22902
Alderman Library   804-924-3021
     University of Virginia, Charlottesville, VA 22903-2498
The Book Gallery   804-977-2892
     1207 Emmet Street, Charlottesville, VA 22903
Jefferson Madison Regional Library   804-979-7151
     201 East Market Street, Charlottesville, VA 22901
New Dominion Book Shop   804-295-252
     404 East Main Street, Charlottesville, VA 22901
Williams Corner Bookstore   804-977-4858
     222 East Main Street, Charlottesville, VA 22901

Local Publications

C'Ville Review   804-295-3986
     P.O. Box 527, Charlottesville, VA 22902
The Daily Progress   804-978-7200
     685 West Rio Road, Charlottesville, VA 22901
The Observer   804-295-0124
     100 South Street West, Charlottesville, VA 22902

Emergency Help
Dial 911

Entertainment and Attractions

Ash Lawn-Highland	804-293-9539
James Monroe Parkway, Charlottesville, VA 22902	
Cabell Hall Box Office/Concert Information	804-924-3984
112 Old Cabell Hall, Charlottesville, VA 22903	
CHALFA (Charlottesville-Albemarle Foundation	
for Encouragement of the Arts)	804-296-9999
Box 3030, Charlottesville, VA 22901	
Charlottesville Performing Arts Center	804-979-9532
1400 Melbourne Road, Charlottesville, VA 22901	
Culbreth/Helms Theaters	804-924-3376
One Culbreth Road, Charlottesville, VA 22903-2486	
Four County Players	804-832-5355
P.O. Box 1, Barboursville, VA 22903	
James River Runners	804-286-2338
Route 4, Box 106, Scottsville, VA 24590	
Jeffersonian Wine Grape Growers Soc. (Vineyard Tour Info)	804-296-4188
Route 5, Box 429, Charlottesville, VA 22901	
Live Arts	804-977-4177
609 East Market Street, Charlottesville, VA 22901	
McGuffey Art Center	804-295-7973
201 Second Street NW, Charlottesville, VA 22901	
Michie Tavern	804-977-1234
Route 21, Box 112, Charlottesville, VA 22902	
Monticello (Tour Info)	804-979-7346
P.O. Box 316, Charlottesville, VA 22902	
Piedmont Council of the Arts (Office)	804-980-3366
P.O. Box 5708, Charlottesville, VA 22905 (Events Info)	804-980-3366
Parks	
Local	
Albemarle Parks and Recreation	804-296-5844
401 McIntire Road, Charlottesville, VA 22902	
Charlottesville Parks and Recreation	804-971-3260
P.O. Box 911, Charlottesville, VA 22902	
National Parks Service	
Shenandoah National Park	703-999-2229
Simmons Gap Ranger Station, Skyline Drive	804-985-7293
University of Virginia (Rotunda) (Events Line)	804-924-3777
Charlottesville, VA 22903 (Tour Info)	804-924-7969
Virginia Discovery Museum (Tour Info)	804-293-5528
P.O. Box 1128, Charlottesville, VA 22902 (Office)	804-977-1025

For Further Reading

Clark, Mizzell. *Crossroads,* (booklet). Charlottesville Savings and Loan Association, 1960s.

The Daily Progress newspaper, Charlottesville, 1970-92.

Heblich, Fred T. and Mary Ann Elwood. *Charlottesville and the University of Virginia.* Norfolk/Virginia Beach: Donning Co., 1982.

Hogan, Pendleton. *The Lawn, A Guide to Jefferson's University.* Charlottesville: The University Press of Virginia, 1987.

Hughes, Sarah S. *Surveyors and Statesmen, Land Measuring in Colonial Virginia.* Richmond: The Virginia Surveyors Foundation, Ltd., and The Virginia Association of Surveyors, Inc., 1979.

Hunter, Robert F. and Edwin L. Dooley, Jr. *Claudius Crozet.* Charlottesville: University Press of Virginia, 1989.

Isaac, Rhys. *The Transformation of Virginia, 1740-1790.* Williamsburg: The Institute of Early American History and Culture, 1982.

Jefferson's Albemarle: A Guide to Albemarle County and the City of Charlottesville, Virginia. Compiled by the workers of the Writers' Program of the Work Projects Administration in the State of Virginia. Charlottesville: Charlottesville and Albemarle County Chamber of Commerce, 1941 (Second edition—Revised.)

Langhorne, Elizabeth Coles, K. Edward Lay, and William D. Rieley. *A Virginia Family and Its Plantation Houses.* Charlottesville: The University Press of Virginia, 1987.

Loth, Calder, ed. *The Virginia Landmarks Register.* Charlottesville: The University Press of Virginia, 1986.

Magazine of Albemarle County History, vols. 1-49. Charlottesville: The Albemarle County Historical Society 1942-1991.

Massey, Don W. *The Episcopal Churches of the Diocese of Virginia.*

Mead, Edward C. *Historic Homes of the Southwest Mountains of Virginia.* Harrisonburg: C.J. Carrier Co., 1978. Copyright 1898, J.B. Lippincott.

Meeks, Steven G. *Crozet: A Pictorial History.* Elkin, Va.: Meeks Ent., 1983.

Mitchell, Richard S. and William F. Giannini. *Minerals of Albemarle County, Virginia.* Va. Div. of Mineral Resources, Publication 89. Charlottesville: Comm. of Virginia, Dept. of Mines, Minerals and Energy, Div. of Mineral Resources, 1988.

Moore, John Hammond. *Albemarle, Jefferson's County, 1727-1976*. Charlottesville: The University Press of Virginia, 1976. (especially Chapter 10: "Turnpikes, Canals and Steam Engines")

Moore, Virginia. *Scottsville on the James*. Charlottesville: Jarman Press, 1969.

O'Neal, William B. *An Official Guide to Four Centuries of Building in the Old Dominion*. New York: Virginia Museum by Walker & Company, Inc., 1968.

Pawlett, Nathaniel Mason, and Edward K. Lay. *Historic Roads of Virginia, Early Road Location: Key to Discovering Historic Resources?* Charlottesville: Va. Hwy. and Transportation Research Council, May 1980.

Pawlett, Nathaniel Mason. *Historic Road of Virginia, Albemarle County Roads, 1725-1816*. Charlottesville, Va. Hwy. and Transportation Research Council, January 1981.

——————. *Historic Roads of Virginia: Albemarle County Road Orders, 1744-1748*. Charlottesville: Va. Hwy. and Transportation Research Council, June 1975.

——————. *Historic Roads of Virginia, Albemarle County Road Orders, 1783-1816*. Charlottesville: Va. Hwy. and Transportation Research Council, December 1975.

——————. *Historic Roads of Virginia, Goochland County Road Orders, 1728-1744*. Charlottesville: Va. Hwy. and Transportation Research Council, June 1975.

Peters, Margaret T., compiler. *A Guidebook to Virginia's Historical Markers*. Charlottesville: The University Press of Virginia, 1985.

Rawlings, Mary. *The Albemarle of Other Days*. Charlottesville: The Michie Company, 1925.

——————. *Ante-Bellum Albemarle*. Charlottesville: The Michie Company, 1925.

Trout, W.E. III *A Guide to the Works of the James River and Kanawha Company from the City of Richmond to the Ohio River*. Richmond: The Virginia Canals and Navigations Society: Second Edition, April 1988.

Woods, Edgar. *Albemarle County in Virginia*. Charlottesville: 1901. (Reprinted, Bridgewater, Va.: The Greek Bookman, 1932.)

Young, Douglas. *A Brief History of the Staunton and James River Turnpike*. Charlottesville: 1976.

Index

About the Author

Susan De Alba agrees with John McPhee that "a sense of where you are" is the only basis for meaningful connection to a place or its people. She studied writing with Clifford Dowdey at the University of Richmond and the Elizabethan world of Virginia's first English settlement at Stratford-upon-Avon's Shakespeare Institute and explores her Virginia roots through her writing. Her essays have appeared in *Commonwealth* magazine, *Albemarle* magazine, *Virginia Business, Miami Magazine* and the *Washington Times* among others. She collects old *Baedekers.*

.... NOTES ....

.... NOTES ....

.... NOTES ....

.... NOTES ....

························· NOTES ·························

Order Information

Order these books
from your favorite bookstore
or directly from

Rockbridge Publishing Company
P.O. Box 70-BK
Natural Bridge Station, VA 24579

Please add 4.5% sales tax in Virginia.
For shipping and handling,
please include $2.50 for the first book or tape
and $1 for each additional item to the same address.

MC/VISA accepted

Phone: (703) 291-1063
Fax: (703) 291-1346

Ask for our free catalog!

Thank you!

Virginia in the Civil War

Also from Rockbridge Publishing Company . . .

JAMES LAWSON KEMPER, Maj. Gen. C.S.A.: THE CONFEDERACY'S FORGOTTEN SON

by Harold R. Woodward, Jr.   *hardcover $21.95*

CSA general, governor of Virginia, attorney, legislator and Mason, Kemper is the ultimate soldier-statesman who based his life on service to his country. Despite a serious wound that left him with lifelong pain, he rebuilt a life sacrificed to the Confederacy, a shining example of Southern tenacity and grace. Too long a footnote in Southern history, this is his only biography. ISBN 0-9623572-7-8

TED BARCLAY, LIBERTY HALL VOLUNTEERS: LETTERS FROM THE STONEWALL BRIGADE

by Charles W. Turner, editor   *hardcover $19.95*

Four years of war recorded by a well-educated young Virginian who lauds Southern leaders and laments the realities of the battlefield in vivid prose. Includes previously unpublished photos and biographical sketches of about 200 comrades and civilians. ISBN 0-9623572-4-3

FOR HOME AND HONOR: THE STORY OF MADISON COUNTY, VIRGINIA, DURING THE WAR BETWEEN THE STATES

by Harold R. Woodward, Jr.   *paperback $18.95*

Madison County, typical of the rural South when candy was a penny and the smell of freshly-ground flour lingered in wagons newly returned from the neighborhood mill, is resurrected in this carefully researched effort. The county was the basic sociologic and commercial unit of the antebellum South, the heart of government and the focal point of daily life. This is the story of the boys who went off to War and what happened when the boys were gone. No ISBN

THE CONFEDERATE CHALLENGE: 1,001 QUESTIONS AND ANSWERS ABOUT THE WAR OF THE REBELLION

by John M. Hightower   *paperback, $10.00*

Super for use with popular TV and board trivia games! Questions organized by category help the reader track down information of special interest. Weapons, battles, music, politics, women and more. *"A delight to historians and the general public"* John McGlone, *Journal of Confederate History.* ISBN 0-9623572-6-X

Virginia in Depth

Also from Rockbridge Publishing Company . . .

COUNTRY ROADS: ROCKBRIDGE COUNTY, VIRGINIA
by Katherine Tennery and Shirley Scott   *paperback; $12.95*
Tour the back roads near Lexington. Detailed maps guide you past manor houses, log cabins, Victorian villages, the soaring Natural Bridge and much, much more! Easy-to-read history for armchair travelers and delightful day trips for visitors. ISBN 0-9623572-0-0

ON TAPE: A RIDE IN THE COUNTRY: LEXINGTON, VIRGINIA
adapted from the Rockbridge guide book, above   *cassette: $9.95*
Whether you're in intrepid trekker or an airmchair traveler, the friendly narrators on this hour-long tape will make you feel welcome as they share local tales and historic gossip and point out interesting sights. Follow the path of the pioneers along the Midland Trail, look for deer and turkeys behind House Mountain, stop at Lake Robertson for a leg-stretcher, then come back to Lexington over Brushy Hill, following the roads used by Hunter's Yankees during the War and General Lee and his faithful Traveller afterward.

LEXINGTON IN OLD VIRGINIA
by Henry Boley   *paperback reprint $16.95*
With photographs by Michael Miley, who was known as General Lee's photographer. This delightful work, first published in 1936, paints a sweeping picture of the times, but also details the pleasures and concerns of everyday life. Nine chapters relate to the Civil War. Personal reflections and stories include town history, Virginia Military Academy, Washington and Lee. Told in an intimate, charming style. ISBN 0-9623572-2-7

GLASGOW, VIRGINIA: 100 YEARS OF DREAMS
by Lynda Mundy-Norris Miller   *hardcover $35.00*
Extraordinary photographs and memories tell the story of "boom towns" all over the Valley of Virginia. At the confluence of the James and Maury rivers, Glasow was a prime target for high-talking 1890s land developers who quickly faded away, leaving the sturdy Scotch-Irish settlers to turn their own dreams into reality. Events come alive with first-hand accounts gleaned from interviews, diaries and family records. Includes old 140 photos. ISBN 0-9623572-5-1